For

STERLING

Tales of Edisto

By

Nell S. Graydon

Photographs
By
CARL JULIEN

Columbia, S.C.
The R. L. Bryan Company
1955

CHARLES E. LEE, PRODUCTION EDITOR

Printed by The R. L. Bryan Company. Illustrations by the
Carolina Engraving Company, Columbia, S.C.

ACKNOWLEDGMENTS

No book becomes a reality without the aid of a number of people. My thanks are due to Charles E. Lee, editor of the University of South Carolina Press, for his unfailing interest and competent help; to S. L. Latimer, Jr., John A. Montgomery, and Eugene B. Sloan, editors of *The State* (Columbia, S.C.), for printing my first stories of Edisto — an encouragement without which this book would not have been written; to Dr. Anne King Gregorie, editor of the *South Carolina Historical Magazine*, for her faith when I was doubtful; and to Mrs. J. C. Self, for suggesting the writing of the book.

I am also grateful to those who gave generously of their time and knowledge, helping me to gather material, or giving permission to photograph their homes: Mrs. Helen Grimball Whaley, Mrs. Lucy Whaley Rast (Mrs. J. H.), Mr. and Mrs. Joseph LaRoche Seabrook, Carl Julien, Mr. and Mrs. William E. Seabrook, Miss Henrietta Seabrook, Mrs. Rachel Whaley Hanckel, Mitchell Seabrook, Mrs. Edwin Belser, Mrs. Arthur F. Langley, Mrs. J. S. Seabrook, Dr. and Mrs. John Townsend, John E. Jenkins, Mrs. Edward Jenkins, Judge Marcellus Whaley, Mrs. George Cullen Battle, Mrs. Frank Wilkenson, Mrs. Virginia Griffen Burns, Dr. and Mrs. L. B. Newell, Colonel George Cornish, Mrs. J. P. Abney, Bishop Albert S. Thomas, Mrs. Donald D. Dodge, Mrs. Lee Mikell, Mrs. Julia Mikell LaRoche, Mr. and Mrs. J. G. Murray, Chalmers S. Murray, Mrs. Marion Seabrook Connor (Mrs. Parker), Dr. and Mrs. Jenkins Pope, Admiral and Mrs. C. D. Murphey, Carew Rice, Percival H. Whaley, Mrs. G. W. Seabrook, Mrs. Mamie Johnston Stevens, Mrs. Willie Mikell, and Captain Teddy Bailey.

John Bennett graciously permitted me to reprint his delightful story, "Revival Pon Top Edisto." Equally kind were Dr. and Mrs. I. Jenkins Mikell in allowing me to use the manuscript, "Rumbling of the Chariot Wheels," by the late Jenkins Mikell. In writing of the churches of the Island, I have relied heavily on the Session Book Minutes of the Presbyterian Church, and for Episcopal history upon the Private Register of Reverend Edward S. Thomas, now in the possession of Bishop Albert S. Thomas. Other material is quoted with the permission of the following newspapers: *The State* and *The State Magazine* (Columbia, S.C.), *The News and Courier* (Charleston, S.C.), *The Press and Standard* (Walterboro, S.C.), *The Baltimore Sun,* and *The New York Sun* (now *The New York World-Telegram and Sun*).

N. S. G.

Contents

Illustrations

(Between pages 54 and 87)

Tales of Edisto

Introduction

FORTY miles southwest of Charleston, South Carolina, within the arms of two tidal rivers, lies a fabulous Island. An aura of mystic and alluring charm hovers over the Island and its old homes. Weird gray moss shrouds with ghostly grandeur the queenly magnolias and gnarled live oaks around the plantation houses. Yellow jessamine and white Cherokee rose give an eerie loveliness to dark tangled jungles of palmetto and myrtle, yucca and jack vine. Tidal marshes stretch wide and lonely, the swaying gray-green grass hiding from view the twists and turns of salt creeks and inlets.

In the stillness of the early evening, the faint haunting melody of a slave lullaby drifting through the twilight, the galloping of a horse passing by, the echo of a footstep, or the swish of a silken skirt can bring forth half-forgotten memories of long ago. Then, if you have been welcomed into the homes and hearts of the Island, you may hear stories of the people and the land.

In the old days, a tribe of Indians called Edistows pitched their tents on the banks of the North Edisto River and found a paradise in the fertile land with its abundant game. Later, the exploring Spaniards called the Island Oristo, still later it was known as Locke, and some original grants give the title as Mause Island; but for many, many years it has been called Edisto.

Some claim that Edisto was settled before Charleston. Old records tell us that the Earl of Shaftesbury, one of the Lords Proprietors, bought the land about 1674 from the Indians for a piece of cloth, hatchets, beads, and other goods; and we know that soon afterwards Paul Grimball had a home at Point of Pines, where the tabby remains of its foundation can still be seen. About 1682, South Carolina's fifth colonial governor, Joseph Morton, built his handsome house on the

(1)

Island and brought slaves in large numbers to Edisto. But the Indians and Spaniards made living there hazardous, and in 1686 the Spaniards raided the Island, burned Grimball's and Morton's houses, and carried away "loot of great value," including silver and slaves.

The first permanent settlers attempted to grow rice on Edisto, but were unsuccessful because of the lack of fresh-water ponds and suitable land. They then turned to the culture of indigo, for which there was a ready and profitable market in England. But with the beginning of the Revolution, Great Britain cut off the bounty she had been paying on indigo, and its cultivation in South Carolina nearly ceased.

At the close of the eighteenth century, the Edisto Island planters discovered a new source of great wealth in Sea Island cotton. The weed flourished in the Island's black fertile soil and produced a long silky staple with so perfect a texture "it was adapted to the most delicate manufacture." In fact, the land produced finer cotton than was made in the Bahamas, from which the first seed for planting in the Sea Islands was procured. It is said that the cotton from the Edisto Island plantations was never put on the market: the mills in France contracted for it before it was put in the ground. Nearly all of the planters made periodic trips abroad and visited the mills using their product. The planters on Edisto experimented with their seed, and after a time each one perfected a jealously guarded strain of his own. It is said that each of them could recognize his own cotton whenever he saw it.

The sale of cotton brought the Edisto Island planters riches beyond their wildest dreams. They sent their sons and daughters to the North and to Europe to be educated. They built elegant homes and ordered fine mahogany and rosewood furniture from abroad. Later, skilled cabinet-makers on the plantations copied many of these pieces; the earlier ones were from the original designs of Hepplewhite, Sheraton, and other famous craftsmen. Sideboards with convex, concave, or serpentine fronts, and three-piece banquet tables of polished mahogany graced their homes. Some of the tables when joined together would seat as many as twenty-four persons. Nearly every dining room had its liquor cabinet (for the old Islanders, while deeply religious, were not tee-totalers). Exquisitely inlaid in satinwood or curly maple, with motifs of holly, acorns, or flowers, the cabinets consisted of square compartments supported on high, slender legs.

Library shelves were lined with handsomely bound books on every known subject. Parlors were furnished with elaborately carved settees and chairs; mirrors in gold-leaf frames hung on the walls, and imported damask draperies decorated the windows. Acres of land surrounding the homes were laid off in gardens and parks, planted with rare shrubs and flowers. Everywhere was evidence of great wealth and luxurious living.

As the planters prospered, they established summer residences on Edingsville, a small barrier island connected to Edisto by a causeway built on a foundation of sea shells and black marsh mud. They acquired town houses in Charleston, where they spent a few weeks each year in a round of social activities, and in the summer they made trips with retinues of servants to Virginia Springs, Newport, and other famous watering places.

It was an idyllic life, and it continued until the beginning of 1861. Then there was war. The cotton fields lay idle; and weeds grew in the old formal gardens. The beautiful houses stood empty; dust settled on the fine velvet and damask upholstery, and spiders spun shimmering webs between crystal prisms on chandeliers. The pendulum was beginning to swing backward.

Among the early settlers were the Chisolms, Middletons, Clarks, Framptons, Baynards, Seabrooks, Hanahans, Townsends, Murrays, Whaleys, Edingses, Mikells, Jenkinses, Wescoats, Mitchells, and Baileys. Their children intermarried, and within a few decades nearly all were connected by blood or marriage. When the Popes came from St. Helena, the Stevenses from Johns Island, and the LaRoches from Wadmalaw, they married into Edisto families, soon becoming Islanders themselves. It has been impossible to write at length about each of these families, but the tales that are told here show the pattern that with little variation applies to them all.

The bulk of the material used in this book has been given me by descendants of the first planters. They told me their stories and let me see their old diaries and family letters. When I have quoted from these documents I have taken care to quote exactly, except for occasionally correcting inadvertent misspelling and modernizing punctuation. The Negroes, too, have contributed their share. I have heard them sing the songs of their forefathers and tell of Drolls, Boo Daddies, Plat Eyes, and other terrible spirits who came back on this earth at certain times to plague the lives of men. The Negroes are an integral part of life on the Island.

Through the years people have come to the Island and gone away to write of what they have seen and heard. Over sixty years ago, a brilliant writer came, hoping to find a story, but "he went away without any clear idea of what to write concerning these people, saying they were too subtle. He likened them in his own mind to the creeks and inlets, as having run along for so long in the same channel, unmixed with other channels, meeting only the same conditions, that they had a way and meaning of their own — the place making them what they were and they making it what it was."

I have not tried to write about the Islanders, but simply to retell the stories as they were told to me. Except for occasionally substituting a name where it could bring embarrassment to those still living, I have made no changes. The story is not mine; it really belongs to the Islanders themselves.

The Planters

The First Mistress of Bleak Hall

EARLY in 1780, the fifth year of the American struggle for independence, the British fleet left its base at Savannah and sailed up the South Carolina coast until it reached the North Edisto River, where troops were landed on John's Island. Part of the fleet proceeded to blockade Charleston harbor, while the troops took possession of John's and James islands and advanced until they were on the bank of the Ashley River opposite the city. In Charleston, preparations for defense were made. The women, children, and aged remaining in the town were advised to seek shelter in the cellars or basements of their homes.

Like many others, the house on Linyard Street appeared deserted. Heavy wooden shutters were tightly closed, and magnolia leaves lay thick on the unswept walk. Bright April sunshine cast shadows in the garden, and the breeze from the sea swayed the large rose and white tipped oleander bushes. The scent of the tender new growth on boxwood plants mingled with the fragrance of banana shrub and tea olive. Bees rejoiced in the abundant sweetness of the spring, and mocking birds in the dense shrubbery chirped happily and undisturbed, as they made their nests of slender, short sticks laid together.

Inside the house, the upper rooms were empty; but down below in the cellar a single candle dimly lit a small, bare room. On a cot lay a young woman with drawn, white face turned in pathetic appeal to two aged Negroes watching by her side. There was no sound except the labored breathing of the sick woman. Once a baby whimpered, and Jean, the old Negress, arose and went to it. With gentle hands she made the child comfortable; then quickly rinsing the small garment and hanging it up to dry, she resumed her seat near the cot of her sick Mistress.

Mrs. Daniel Jenkins of Edisto Island, come to Charleston to spend a few weeks with her husband, a captain in the American forces, lay dying. Stricken by illness, her husband recently captured by the British, and her way cut off by the enemy, Mrs. Jenkins had entrusted herself and her child to the care of her two aged servants.

As the hours went by, the sick woman's condition grew steadily worse, and her mind wandered. Then she imagined herself back on Edisto Island with her little son, who had been left there with relatives. At times in her delirium, the child's father was there, too, and she was remembering their first meeting — the days of their courtship, when they rode through shady lanes, stopping to gather the yellow jessamine she loved. Then, she was living over the wedding and all the happiness that followed it. Once she dreamed she was making tiny clothes, carefully stitching the dainty material in just the way Maum Jean had taught her to make doll dresses when she was a little girl.

Then, at last, her mind cleared, and she moaned as a spasm of pain left her limp and exhausted. "Jack," she whispered — and the old Negro man bent low to catch the words — "take my little girl home, and tell Daniel his mother sends him her love, and tell him to be a good boy." Her pale lips moved again, but no sound came from them, and she seemed to be looking past the slaves at the doorway leading to the stairs. For a moment there were tears in her eyes, and then they slowly closed. As the restless hands grew still, great shuddering sobs burst from the old Negroes.

Night drew near, and Jack, followed closely by Jean, climbed the cellar stairs into the upper part of the house. Passing by the front entrance, where but a week ago Captain Jenkins had reluctantly bid goodbye to his wife, they proceeded up the winding stairs, their footsteps making no sound on the thick velvet carpet. In the attic, the slaves dragged a large oaken dower chest from under the eaves. Opening it, Jean removed fine handwoven sheets, and from another box she took a soft silken quilt, with which Jack carefully lined the heavy chest. Then, between them they dragged the dower chest down to the cellar and tenderly placed the quiet form in it. Out in the garden the old man dug a temporary grave, and in the gloom of the night the sorrowing slaves buried their young Mistress.

Their grim work done, the Negroes moved swiftly, preparing to carry out Mrs. Jenkins' request to take her baby to Edisto Island. The waterway, they decided, was safer than the closely guarded highway. Jack, who had been born on the coast, had made the trip many times in a large boat as a member of the crew. He was familiar with the currents and the landmarks and had no fear of losing the way. While he gathered up food and filled a bottle with water, Jean hurriedly tore a clean linen sheet into small squares, and putting a spoonful of sugar mixed with a tiny bit of butter into each, tied it securely with a thread. These morsels, called "sugar tits" by the Negroes and loved by babies, would give the child a little nourishment and keep it quiet on the trip.

When they were ready to leave the house, the baby was warmly wrapped and securely fastened to Jean's back. In utter darkness, the two faithful slaves slipped silently into the night. At times, they crawled like cats on the ground. Again, they darted from tree to tree. Finally, they reached the water, where in a secluded spot a small "paddlin'" boat was hid.

In the Exchange Building in Charleston, a short distance from Linyard Street, two men talked in guarded tones. Captain Daniel Jenkins paced the floor with his hands clasped behind his back, and Colonel Isaac Hayne sat on an upturned wooden keg and looked with compassion at the man with whom he had shared the room since the two of them had been captured by the British. From the incessant firing outside, the men knew the besiegers had almost taken the city, and Captain Jenkins was consumed with fear concerning the fate of his wife. He was confident that the two servants who had been given Mrs. Jenkins by her father, Jonathan Frampton, would protect her at the risk of their own lives, but they would be helpless if taken prisoners. The British were dealing harshly with the Negroes captured in the Low Country; hundreds of them had been carried to barren Otter Island, across the river from Edisto, and left there to die of exposure and starvation. This was worry enough. Captain Jenkins tried not to think of a rumored outbreak of smallpox in the town, or what would happen to his wife if the two slaves left with her should be stricken with the disease.

So the long days and nights, filled with forebodings and uncertainty, passed slowly. Death itself seemed easier to face than the torture that imagination brought to the unhappy prisoner. It would be many weeks before Captain Jenkins learned of the loss of his wife.

At daybreak, on the morning following Mrs. Jenkins' death, the boat containing the two Negroes and the baby anchored in a cove many miles from Charleston. During the day, several British scouting parties passed nearby, but the tall marsh grass made a thick screen, and the fugitives were not discovered. The sun went down and a gray mist encircled the boat, but Jack did not dare to take it into the open water while there was a ray of light.

As twilight faded into night, the boat moved out of the cove. Dark clouds were in the sky, and a brooding wind brought lines of worry to the old man's face. A few drops of rain began to fall, and the wind blew stronger. Sometimes it tipped the boat or turned it sideways, dipping a little water; but each time the Negro managed to straighten it.

During lulls in the wind, he glanced anxiously at his wife and the bundle which she held so carefully in her arms, expecting any second to see them swept overboard. Each passing minute seemed to make the journey more hazardous, and he hardly dared hope to reach the Island. The baby stirred and gave a feeble wail. The woman began to sing softly; it was more a prayer than a song. As if in answer, the sea calmed, and little by little the boat made way in the darkness. A higher power surely guarded the lives of the helpless child and the two old Negroes; for a few hours later, hungry and shivering with cold, they reached home. Thus Hephzibah Jenkins came to Edisto Island.

The large boat, manned by twelve slaves, all experienced and well-trained oarsmen, skimmed rapidly over the water as it rode the incoming tide. The black men gazed sorrowfully at their Master seated in the boat; at times his face was bowed upon his knees; again he stared fixedly at the shoreline. It was a sad homecoming for him.

The boat moved into the mouth of the North Edisto River, past familiar banks covered with woods and thick undergrowth. Only the swish of the oars as they cut the water broke the stillness. Rounding a curve, the travelers saw the wharf, and it seemed to Captain Jenkins that all his relatives and neighbors were there to greet him. His glance moved rapidly over the crowd until he found the two he sought. When the boat scraped the landing, without waiting for it to make fast he jumped ashore and, with a sob, took his two children in his arms.

Captain Jenkins, being young and eligible, in the course of time married Benjamin Seabrook's daughter, Martha. If in the years that followed, the fragrance of yellow jessamine, caught unexpectedly, brought him memories, sweet and poignant, of one who was once dearer to him than life, no one ever knew; for he apparently had found complete happiness again.

II

Hephzibah Jenkins was like her mother — soft black hair framing a face with deep-set eyes, small regular features, and a tender, smiling mouth. Early in her life, it became apparent that she was gifted with a brilliant mind, a strong will, and a great sense of justice. Yet although her numerous relatives on the Island pampered the motherless girl, she remained lovable and unspoiled.

Daniel Townsend, a friend of Hephzibah's father, watched her grow to womanhood and admired the young girl's quiet dignity and force of character. When she was sixteen years of age, he went to Captain Jenkins. "I love your daughter," he said frankly, "and if I am able to win her love and your consent to our marriage, I will do my best to make her happy." He evidently pleaded his cause well, for before a year had passed, he and Hephzibah were married. They lived at Bleak Hall, "so called from proximity to the gales of the great Atlantic just a mile away." Mr. Townsend developed the plantation until it was one of the most productive on the Carolina coast.

Botany Bay or Island, a part of the Bleak Hall plantation, has been known by various names — Tucker Island, Watch Island, and Clark's Bay. Once it was large and covered with thick woods, but through the years the ocean has encroached on the land until now there is only a strip of almost treeless beach, cut off from the large plantation by inlet, and a small island known as "Porky," a name shortened from "Pourquoi." To the right is Frampton Inlet, running between Botany Island and Edingsville. Many tales have been told of smugglers and pirates landing along this part of the coast.

Hephzibah and her brother Daniel were unusually devoted to each other. The loss of their mother seemed to give the boy a deep feeling of responsibility for his sister. When Bleak Hall was completed, Mr. Townsend insisted that young Daniel make his home there; and the older man often remarked that he loved the handsome, genial youth like a son. Daniel was encouraged to invite his friends for long visits, and Mr. Townsend took part in many of their "hunts." On March 16, 1804, following one of these hunts, a great sorrow came to Bleak Hall.

Daniel had just purchased a large, open boat, and he decided to take his guests down the coast to Beaufort in it. The crew, composed of twelve of his finest slaves, was overjoyed at the prospect. The sky was clear that March morning, and the tip of a sun showing on the far horizon gave promise of perfect weather. The young men were frisky as colts as they joked together and eagerly looked forward to the trip. Hephzibah watched the vessel leave the wharf, its shiny new paint gleaming in the rays of the rising sun. But a few minutes after she had turned homeward, the boat in going out Frampton Inlet "struck a bank and upset." Slaves working on Edingsville, hearing the cries of the Negro men as they sank beneath the waves, quickly went for help.

A large crowd soon gathered, but a sudden squall had turned the tranquil sea into a raging torrent, and a screen of darkness hung over the little island. Occasionally, a screaming white sea gull gleamed against the inky-blue of the sky as the wind helped it wing its way to land and safety, but the thick mist that hung over the ocean was a gray impenetrable mass. Numerous attempts were made to launch a boat, but each one failed as huge waves broke and filled the boats with water. The people could only watch and pray as they stood among the sand dunes and looked helplessly toward the sea.

As suddenly as it came the storm ceased, and brilliant sunshine shone over the water. A cry went up from the people as they saw an object floating in the distance, and as it came nearer the watchers could see a man clinging to a fragment of wreckage. Eager hands brought him ashore. It was Henry Bailey, the "sole survivor of the tragedy." Benjamin Scott of St. Helena Island, Mr. Wood of Beaufort, John Bailey, Daniel Jenkins, Jr., and his two half-brothers, Richard and Thomas Jenkins, and the twelve Negroes — all were drowned. Hephzibah was among the last to leave the sad scene. Daniel was an excellent swimmer, and she hoped against hope that he had managed to reach land. It was nearly dark when his body was found, washed ashore far down the beach.

The drowning of her beloved brother was a great shock to Hephzibah. It was hard for her to realize that the gay, fun-loving youth who had told her a laughing goodbye such a short time ago would not brighten her home again. She never ceased to miss him, and even when she was an old woman there were times when the sound of a gay laugh would bring memories of him and cause her heart to beat faster and tears to fill her eyes.

III

Mr. Townsend sat by the fire, pretending to read his paper but glancing every few minutes over it at Hephzibah. Hephzibah did not raise her eyes from the embroidery she held in her hand, but her needle jabbed the linen violently with each stitch. The air was tense with unspoken words. Mr. Townsend was the first to break. Unable to endure the silence any longer, he threw his paper aside, arose, and walked the length of the large room twice before he stopped in front of his wife.

"Hephzibah, I have had enough of this foolishness. I will not change my will."

"But Daniel, it is not fair to the other children. I cannot bear that they should be left with only a few slaves, and their brother, because he happens to be the eldest, inherit the bulk of the estate."

"Our forefathers considered it a good plan that the estate should descend to the eldest son, so why do you wish to change a custom that has been accepted in our family for generations?"

"Perhaps it is time for a change," his wife retorted as she left the room.

The following day, Hephzibah arose early and went to Shargould, a plantation she had inherited from her brother Daniel. There she gave orders to have her slaves immediately start the construction of a house on Frampton Inlet Creek.

When the house was completed she moved into it despite Mr. Townsend's anger. Not until her husband decided to include all their children in the distribution of the property did she return to Bleak Hall.

Hephzibah's house was burned nearly ninety years ago, but its tabby foundation remains — a sturdy monument to one woman's indomitable will.

Hephzibah's determination was again displayed when the Baptist Church was erected. Hephzibah's father was an Episcopalian, a vestryman and a trustee of the fund subscribed for the "support of a minister." Mr. Townsend was an elder in the Presbyterian Church and active in its support. Despite the example of father and husband, Hephzibah was a staunch Baptist. In the early days there were some Baptists among several families who came to Edisto from the colony on Port Royal, and it may be that Hephzibah grew up under the influence of a Baptist relative. Her husband insisted that she should worship in either the Presbyterian or Episcopal Church, but Hephzibah wanted her denomination to have its own building.

When Mr. Townsend refused to contribute to the church fund his wife proposed to raise, Hephzibah had an enormous tabby oven built. Here she ordered the servants to bake cookies in large numbers and sell them from a roadside stand. This was too much for Mr. Townsend, and he forbade the slaves to have anything to do with the project. But when his wife countered by saying that she herself would bake the cookies and peddle them, he knew she meant exactly what she said, and he withdrew his objection. The church was built largely through Hephzibah's effort, and it seems that she had entire control of it.

In 1841, while a new Episcopal Church was being erected, Hephzibah graciously invited the members to worship in the Baptist Church until their edifice was completed, and as an expression of their appreciation, the Episcopalians set apart a pew in the new church for "Mrs. Townsend's use during her lifetime."

When Hephzibah died she was buried in the Baptist churchyard. She had deeded the property to the Baptists on Edisto Island, with the stipulation that it remain under the authority of the Charleston Baptists and never be sold or used for any other purpose. Most of the Edisto Island people are affiliated with either the Presbyterian or Episcopal Church, and in time the only Baptists on the Island were Negroes, who acquired the church. In the churchyard there stands a tall marble shaft, and beneath it rests the mortal remains of Hephzibah Jenkins Townsend. An iron fence encloses her grave, and surrounding it are the graves of dozens of her former slaves.

The Townsends

IN THE nineteenth century Edisto Island plantations passed from one generation to another, like family silver, heirloom furniture, and pride in heredity. Bleak Hall remained in the Townsend family one hundred and thirty-five years. Hephzibah and Daniel's son John, who inherited it, married Mary Caroline Jenkins, and she has left many letters depicting the life there during the 1850's and the terrible days after the Confederate War.

Bleak Hall became renowned for its hospitality and magnificent gardens. While John Townsend was in Columbia, the capital of the state, as Speaker of the House, he met his old friend Dr. James Morrow of Willington, who had just returned from Japan where he had gone as a member of Commodore Perry's expedition. When Mr. Townsend mentioned he was looking for a gardener, Dr. Morrow told of an expert Chinese botanist who had come to America with Perry to care for the rare plants brought from the Far East. But Oqui was not satisfied in Washington; the climate did not suit him, and he was making plans to return to his native land. Perhaps the warmer air of Carolina would tempt him to stay in America.

Mr. Townsend made a special trip to Washington, and Oqui agreed to come to Bleak Hall, where a house called "Celestials," modeled on his old home, was built for him. The slaves worked well under him, and vast sums were spent to make the garden a beautiful place. The lovely white poppies that grow so luxuriantly on the islands along the South Carolina coast were first planted by Oqui's hand. He also brought the yellow-blossomed Chinese tobacco plant, whose trumpet-shaped flower is a magnet for humming birds. He planted camphor, olive, and spice trees and bordered the large vegetable garden at Bleak Hall with sweet oranges. A house was built to store the oranges, with shelves filled with white beach sand along the walls, where the fruit could be buried and kept for months. It was not unusual for Oqui to gather over a thousand oranges from one tree.

All the plantations grew oranges. There were two varieties, sweet and "sour." The sour ones should really be called bitter, for the rind tastes like quinine. These were used to make preserves and marmalades. On Coosau Island, about twenty miles down the coast, there are a few of these sour oranges still bearing fruit. It must have been a fairyland on Edisto when the trees were covered with the delicately textured blooms and their fragrance pervaded the Island.

Oqui took great pride and personal interest in the Bleak Hall garden. Mrs. Townsend, in June, 1858, wrote her daughter Phoebe, a student at Barhamville Female College near Columbia: "We go out every morning when the sun is not too warm and walk in the garden. The spring flowers have disappeared. We have now gardenias, myrtles, and mimosa in bloom, with pomegranates, and golden coreopsis.

I intend to send you a little heliotrope and rose-geranium from Oqui's hot bed. Oqui will have the horrors when he sees the horses carried through the garden to be watered. It is so dry the water elsewhere is not good."

II

Bleak Hall constantly overflowed with guests. The delicious food served on heavy silver dishes or the frailest of French china became a tradition. The large house stood three stories high with a roomy cupola on top. The cupola was added after the house was built so that a homesick bride of one of the Townsends could look across the river to her former home on Wadmalaw Island.

Despite the lengthening shadows of war the Townsends, like the majority of the planters, refused to take its threat seriously. The delusion that they and their children and their children's children would go on forever in their pleasant way of life was deep-rooted. At the beginning of war, a resident of the Island wrote: "Volunteers were called for three months service — they would not be needed longer, the war would be won by then. The Artillery company of Edisto, organized as a pastime, was ordered to the duty of repelling the invaders. With its thirty-odd men and two shining brass muzzle loading cannon — or was it only one? — they left their gun shed and marched the five miles to their post. I do not know but what most, if not all, of them rode in their buggies. At any rate, they finally arrived. They made camp, or at least their body servants did, and then sat down to a two hour dinner. It was really too bad but as it was so late in the afternoon it was scarcely worth while to begin soldiering until the next day. The next day began with a dispute with the Officer of the Day as to who should walk sentry during meals. This was compromised by no one doing sentry duty at that time. All congratulated each other on the happy settlement of that dilemma. Orders from Headquarters were then read. In brief 'sink every ship attempting to cross the bar.' The men gave three cheers and took a drink."

Yet when the grim reality of war did come there were no braver soldiers than these pampered sons of wealth. Many laid down their lives in glory, and those who came back returned with records any man would be proud to claim.

One day in November, 1861, a messenger rode in haste from house to house. The steamboat "Beauregard," sent by the Confederate government, was docked at the public landing, and the messenger carried an order for all those remaining on the Island to evacuate. There was no time to gather up precious possessions and no means of taking them away. With only what they could carry, the planters' families left their homes. An attempt was made to hide valuable silver and china. Some of it was saved, but fortunes were carried away or destroyed by Freedmen and the Federals. When the Townsends returned to Bleak Hall in 1866 they found their home occupied by Negroes. Fine furniture and other property had been wantonly destroyed.

There were many formalities to observe before Colonel Townsend could begin to plant his ravished land: Articles of Agreement with the colored laborers; papers from the Headquarters Assistant Commissioner, Bureau Refugees, Freedmen and Abandoned Lands, restoring his property; and last, the signing of that document that meant the passing forever of a way of life: "I, John Townsend of the County of Charleston, State of South Carolina, do solemnly swear in the presence of Almighty God, that I will henceforth faithfully support and defend the Constitution of the United States and the Union of the States thereunder, and that I will, in like manner, abide by and faithfully support all laws and proclamations which have been made during the existing rebellion with reference to the Emancipation of Slaves."

On December 20, 1867, Colonel Townsend wrote to his son John, a student at South Carolina College, and told him of trouble he had with the Negroes. The letter gives a vivid picture of some of the trials the planter encountered after the

Negroes were freed: "I have had within the last three weeks a somewhat alarming occurrence to take place here; which has greatly annoyed me and given me very constant anxiety to detect the villians. On the night of the second of December my mill was broken open whilst I was in Charleston, by boring out the bolt of the lock with a large auger. The burglars then went up into the loft of the mill, where a large quantity of cotton was spread upon the floor and stole, what was we judge, from 1600 to 2000 lbs. of cotton. This they carried to a boat which they had landed about 300 yards at the back of the mill, at the outlet of the large drain at Ishmails flats (near where the negroes planted their corn this year). Previously to leaving the mill an attempt was made to burn it down — first by throwing lighted matches upon the bulk of the cotton which was spread upon the floor of the loft, from one end to the other. The fire spread over the cotton the length of the building in close contact with the shingles and yet the building did not take fire. They next attempted to burn the mill in the lower story by kindling a bunch of lightwood, split into small pieces and mixed with ginned cotton, to make it more combustible, this was put in contact with the partition between the grist mill and cotton gin rooms. After the lightwood had burned about half length of partition, it went out.

"The boat seems to have been a pretty large one, well manned. At first we supposed that the boat carried the cotton to Charleston but from slight indications which I have received I think it was carried in the direction of the Public Landing and Estate of Murrays and Estate of Edings plantation. Upon the strength of this I procured a search warrant to search Jacobs' (my former sub-driver) house. There I found a great deal of cotton which resembled so much my superfine cotton and some of it in a bag marked in my own private mark (J. T.) that Mr. Lancaster (overseer), who accompanied the constable and myself, did not hestitate to pronounce the cotton to be mine which was stolen."

The following year Colonel Townsend wrote to his son: "My cotton has just been sold for $2.00 per pound. We came to Charleston on 'The Pilot Boy' which now makes one trip each week to Edisto (on Thursday, returning Saturday) taking only 3½ hours from wharf to wharf. My crop this year will pay expenses and leave me a margin of profit to almost make up the losses of the past two years. I shall have no food to buy except meat and molasses for the laborers — having made corn, pease and potatoes enough for my purpose."

At this time, Colonel Townsend's plantation was producing, in spite of the instability of labor, about fifty bales of superfine cotton, and it was bringing double the amount paid for the best West Indian cotton. When he refused to sell any of his seed to a "French Spinner," the man managed to salvage about two handfuls from the cotton shipped to him from Bleak Hall and to send it to the most successful planter in St. Vincent. In consequence, Colonel Townsend had a law passed in South Carolina "where no seed could be exported," with the result that Florida and Georgia could not renew their seed, a handicap that helped drive cultivation out of the states. This, of course, was not Colonel Townsend's intention; he was trying to help not only himself but also his neighbor.

While all the plantations successfully produced the famous Sea Island cotton, Bleak Hall seemed to be unusually well adapted to its culture. Mrs. Townsend wrote on November 24, 1871: "Pa is still picking cotton, his fields benefitted by the frost, while his neighbors are effectually killed." With the coming of the destructive boll weevil, the planting of Sea Island cotton practically ceased on Edisto Island. Unhappily, many fortunes were lost before the planters realized that here was another enemy they could not defeat.

III

In the years immediately following the Confederate War "fishing smacks whose crews were made up of every nationality would sail their two-masted schooners into port at night without any range lights and make harbor in the North Edisto River." Their crews would take shotguns and go through the woods of Botany Bay hunting Colonel Townsend's hogs and cattle. The animals were killed and butchered, and the meat divided. Sometimes Mr. Townsend would try to catch them, but the men "who were little better than old-time pirates" thought that it added zest to the hunt for them to be the hunted. It was a dangerous thing to try to capture one of them, for they were a lawless lot.

Few people know that salt was manufactured off Botany Bay and Townsend Creek used as one of the evaporating ponds. A very old diary tells that "William Mellichamp, a French refugee, in the spring of 1724 seeing the possibilities in manufacture of salt petitioned Governor's Council, for the exclusive right of salt manufacture in Province of South Carolina."

The process used by Mellichamp was very simple. "The salt was run in shallow iron pans, some being as large as 10 by 20 feet. By use of evaporation basins and troughs, water was let in from the ocean in the process of sluices and transferred from one basin to another, as various steps in the process was necessary until the salt finally crystalized. The crystal salt was shovelled into heaps to dry, after which it was pounded fine. The warm climate of South Carolina was peculiarly adapted to salt making.

"Mr. Mellichamp was granted a private monoply on manufacturing salt for a period of five years — also a monoply on sale of all salt sold in the Province. On July 8, 1731, he reported 14,000 bushels of salt had been manufactured. In addition he was granted a bounty of 12 pence currency for every bushel he produced as long as the price did not exceed 10 shillings per bushel." There is no record in the diary of the length of time Mellichamp manufactured salt off Botany Bay.

Bleak Hall, like all the Island plantations, abounds in legends. Take, for instance, the one of Jacob's well. It stands in the "Big Woods" and many bridle paths run near it. Probably, it was a trysting place for lovers in the long ago, and even now it is picturesque and inviting. A wall of tabby surrounds the well, and "Jacobus Fecit" is cut in one side; the crumbling top is steeple-shaped. Here, it is said, a little gray man stands on guard to keep the water pure and to let only "quality" drink its cooling draughts.

Another story tells of the old cemetery on the plantation. It is in the fork of the road, about a mile from Jacob's well, where the road to the right turns toward Bleak Hall and the other leads to Sea Cloud, sometimes called "Seabrook's Folly." When you leave a clearing and enter a narrow road bordered on both sides by dense undergrowth and trees you are near the cemetery. It is then the first wave of hot air hits the back of your neck. You feel it again and again until you leave the area. You have come in contact, so the Negroes say, with Hag's breath, and if you linger in the vicinity she will cast a terrible spell that may even cause death.

There are other stories of Bleak Hall — some gay — and some sad ones better left untold. Among the sad ones is the tale of a Portuguese, with large gold earrings and a red bandana worn turban-fashion on his head, who roams the shores of Botany Bay. One day seven of his victims were found where he had buried them — standing straight up in the sand.

A few decades ago Bleak Hall, now called Botany Bay, was sold; and the house, the second to stand on the site, was torn down and a modern one erected nearby. Tall straight pines grow over the old cotton fields. There are traces of the original garden, and in recent years beautiful camellias and azaleas have been planted. Oqui's poppies and narcissus bloom with unchanging beauty. The warm southern sun that

(23)

caresses the land before sinking in a sky of red, gold, and blue — the ebbing tide — and the fragrance of the rain-kissed earth — remain the same. Timeless, too, is the moonlight that shines off Botany Bay, crowning with silver the top of each dancing wave as on the night Daniel Townsend brought his lovely bride to Bleak Hall.

The Whaleys

ON ITS way to the sea the beautiful South Edisto River flows near the site of Old Dominion plantation house. Like the colorful people who lived there, the mansion has faded into the past, but at one time a glimpse of its gleaming white columns, in a frame of gray-bearded oaks, could be had from the river. Slave quarters stretched for nearly a mile along the bank of the South Edisto. The owner placed them there to give his slaves the benefit of the cool breezes that came up the river from the sea and tempered the scalding heat of summer nights. On each side of the "big house" and behind it were gardens that reached to the edge of the gold-bringing cotton fields. From the house a wide crushed-shell driveway led to a long wharf resting on palmetto logs and protruding into the water. Here cotton was loaded and steamboats anchored.

During the 1820's and for years afterwards Edward Whaley lived at Old Dominion. The Whaley men, reputedly, were brave, fiery tempered, and highly educated; many of them were graduated from Princeton and Harvard. Some were doctors or lawyers as well as planters. From a member of the family I heard the story of Edward Whaley and his wife, Abigail Baynard. Their courtship was a tempestuous one, for Mr. Whaley arrogantly swept all opposition away. Some say he even challenged one persistent rival to a duel. Eligible young men from Charleston and Edisto were in competition for Abigail's favor at the time Edward came home from two years abroad. When he left Edisto, she had been an adolescent girl; he returned to find her the loveliest woman he had ever seen. Beautiful women in many lands had smiled on Edward and maneuvered for introductions to both him and his bank account. He had found none so fair as this girl from a neighboring plantation.

Edward Whaley reached home one bright summer day and went immediately to Edingsville to join his family. That afternoon as he walked along the seashore a group of young people on horseback passed by. Abigail rode a little in front of the others. For a second her eyes met his and then indifferently looked away. While Edward did not recognize the girl, he was confident he had seen her before; but he could not remember the time or place.

Abigail reined in her horse and asked one of her friends, "Do you know the gentleman we just passed?"

The boy laughed and teasingly said, "Now, Gail, don't tell me you didn't recognize the famous globe-trotter, Edward Whaley?"

Abigail was unusually quite the rest of the afternoon. On reaching home, she dismounted, left her horse with a servant, and ran quickly up the steps to the wide veranda. She found her mother and father deep in conversation with Mr. Whaley. "Of course, you know Gail," said her mother.

"This is a surprise!" said Edward, and he took the slender hand in his own.

From that time on he never looked twice at another woman. His whirlwind courtship of Abigail is a legend in the family. Timid suitors withdrew from the field; others more determined found Abigail unresponsive to their suits, and finally they, too, accepted defeat.

The wedding was the most glamorous the Island had ever known. Steamboats loaded with guests docked at the private wharves. A week before the wedding the big plantation houses on Edisto were filled. Dinings and dances that lasted until the early morning were daily occurrences. The bride's trousseau came from France — gowns, chemises, and pantalets, exquisitely stitched and embroidered by the nuns. The heavy satin wedding gown, bearing the label of a famous Parisian designer, would stand alone; and the gossamer veil, fragile as cobwebs, had taken ten women six months to make. It is said that the thread they used came from the famous Sea Island cotton grown on Edisto. It was all like a fairy tale come true.

At the end of a long honeymoon the couple settled at Old Dominion, and in quick succession Abigail bore her husband seven sons. Then a little girl was born; and the mother died. People say that he never smiled after her death. Although he had wealth beyond even this fabulous Island's idea of wealth, it meant little to him when she was not there to share it. On the marble slab above her grave he had inscribed: "He whom thou didst honor with thy friendship erects this frail monument as a momento of his attachment." So a love story ended, leaving only sadness and bitterness and broken dreams.

On the day of his wife's death Edward Whaley carried the new-born baby to his wife's sister, Mrs. Mitchell, who lived on Frogmore Plantation, and without a backward glance at its tiny face, departed. Once each year for nine years he reappeared at Frogmore, and after placing a check for $5,000 on a table, walked out of the house without asking to see his child.

Mrs. Mitchell named the child Abigail. Just after the little girl passed her ninth birthday, Mr. Whaley made a trip to the North. Soon after his return, a coach driven by a liveried man, whose every effort barely succeeded in keeping the four glistening black horses under control, pulled up in front of the Frogmore plantation house. The footman delivered a note from Mr. Whaley ordering his daughter and her nurse to be ready on the morrow for a trip to Baltimore, where he was taking them to enter Abigail in school. Next day a weeping little girl left the only home she had ever known.

Ten dreary years dragged by. While Edward Whaley watched his seven sons grow to manhood, no woman except servants entered Old Dominion. Then word came from the convent in Baltimore: Abigail had completed her education, and would Mr. Whaley send instructions and an escort to take the young lady home? So a gracious, smiling young woman, not unlike her mother, returned to the Island. One wonders if there was sadness behind her smile, and if she thought of the frightened, sobbing child who had gone away. Her brothers welcomed her, and by turns teased, spoiled, and loved her. To her father she brought both comfort and pain. For Edward Whaley, this girl, with her lovely face and unforgettable name, was a constant reminder of a love stronger than death.

II

When each of his children married, Edward Whaley's wedding gift was a plantation. One son received Windsor, the spacious old house that stands fronting Russel Creek on Little Edisto. For many generations afterwards it was the home of a branch of the Whaley family.

Windsor has been the scene of much lavish entertainment. It is told that for one festive occasion the Mistress of Windsor ordered malaga grapes from Spain to entwine among the smilax that decorated its stairway. The light from hundreds of candles gleamed from the massive crystal chandeliers hanging from ceilings decorated with acanthus leaves. Above wide fireplaces, Italian marble mantles stood in rooms so large that it seems impossible that the occupants kept warm, even in Edisto's mild winters.

Richard Harding Davis was entertained at Windsor when he came to write his account of the storm of 1893, one of the worst that ever hit the South Carolina coast. Mr. Davis was so charmed with the household and the Island that he lingered for days after his mission was completed, and said goodbye only when business forced his return to New York.

Mr. Swinton Whaley, who lived at Windsor at the time, one day took Mr. Davis to see a relative, Colonel E. M. Whaley. They found the old planter seated under a large tree in front of his house, with two fat horses tied nearby. The men talked of planting and the old days on the Island — of duels fought and won, and of cotton that brought $2.00 per pound. Finally, the visitor, unable to conceal his curiosity any longer asked, "Why do you keep those two horses tied to the fence?"

"Oh!" came the reply. "I keep them ready there each day in case anybody should happen along to plough for me. I shall be very glad to have my cotton ploughed if anybody comes today."

In writing of the old gentleman, Mr. Davis said: "He lived in his books, of which the house was full, and the farm work went on as it could. He would make no contracts with the Negroes. If at any time he wanted a thing planted or hoed or harvested and the Negroes appeared to do it, they would be paid for the work, otherwise it could go so."

Mr. J. Swinton Whaley, the last member of his family to live at Windsor, "never gave up hope that the famous Sea Island cotton would again bring prosperity back to Edisto Island, and as long as he lived he planted a small patch of seed cotton."

A gruesome tale is told of a happening on Windsor during the early days of slave trading. It was customary on the Island for the planters to isolate for a period all slaves who had come directly from their native country. This quarantine was to protect the plantation from disease — especially cholera. Once three strapping black Negroes, said to have been captured in Haiti and smuggled to the South Carolina coast, were sold to the Master of Windsor. Wood, food, and cooking utensils were placed along with them in the "isolation house." One day a sickening odor reached the slaves working in a nearby field, and the driver or overseer reported it to his Master. An investigation was ordered, and when the door of the house was unlocked, there were found to be only two occupants. The bones of the third were scattered over the room.

During the storm of 1893, Little Edisto was almost completely covered with water. A two-masted schooner dragged her anchor across the Island, striking a house of one of the Whaleys' servants and causing five children, who had climbed on the roof to escape the rising flood waters, to fall into the water and drown.

Mr. Arthur Whaley had charge of the commissary that stood in a corner of the crossroads about two miles from Windsor. A few days after the storm, Mundy, a former slave of the Whaleys, came into the store. The old Negro, then in his ninety-first year, sat down on a wooden bench near the stove. He didn't say anything after his first greeting of "Mornin' Suh"; but Mr. Whaley knew what was expected. He took a large piece of butts meat out of a barrel, filled a bag with corn meal, poured a quart bottle full of black molasses, and gave them all to Mundy.

Mundy said, "E ferget de ker'sene."

While he was drawing the kerosene from a barrel, Mr. Whaley asked, "How is Sue? I haven't seen her since the storm."

"E dead," said the old man.

"Dead? When did she die? I saw her last week."

"Enty, e dead Suh. E binnah pon top ole boat. De water git high'n de boat e gwin' sink. We'uns too heavy. Sue, she ole, ain't bery good cook fur long time. I tink bout t'ain't no use we'un both die den I puts out muh han en tech Sue's back e fall en duh wat'er. Yes suh, Marse Arthur, Sue e dead."

There are other plantations on Edisto that were once owned by the Whaleys. Among them are The Neck, Crawfords, Four Chimneys (now called Old House), and Pine Baron. I have heard the last called Pine Barrens, and I have thought that it may have been Pine Barony in the beginning. It was here one of the Whaley men brought a daughter of Governor Francis Pickens as his bride before going to live at Greenspoint plantation, left him by his grandfather.

Maria Whaley who lived at Pine Baron in the 1850's was sent to a private school in Charleston and was married there, without her father's consent, to George Morris. A relative of Mr. Morris' has described the wedding in her diary.

"George made himself acceptable to Miss Maria Whaley of Edisto, a little young lady still at school, fat and fair with black eyes and charming teeth, a very pretty person. Her father would not hear of the match, George Morris was so much older than his daughter — besides he personally disliked him. Maria consented to leave school where she was finishing her education in Charleston and marry George in St. Michael's church. All his family who were in the city were brought to the church to give respectability to the ceremony which was performed at night by a few dim lights. The bride came in the carriage with Mr. G——'s mother and her bridesmaid, Miss Sarah Seabrook. They walked up the aisle and entered within, the Rev. Dr. Dalcho read the service, and we all stood outside the railing with the look of people who had no business to be there. After it was over the bride was kissed and carried out to the carriage waiting for her and returned to school. The night had become rainy, and in her agitation walking through the garden up to Mrs. Hanburn's door she slipped and got herself wet and muddied so on her arrival Mrs. Hanburn became uneasy lest she should get cold and overlooked her being out late.

"The next morning when George called at the door and asked for Mrs. Morris, the poor startled school mistress thought the man must be mad. When it was explained to her Miss Maria had been married the evening before Mrs. Hanburn fell into screaming hysterics.

"Colonel Whaley was furious, he sent challenges all around and showed himself terrible incensed, but provided the disobedient Maria with money, for he could not bear that his daughter should be dependent on anyone."

I had an unusual experience at Pine Baron in August, 1945. Our cottage on the beach was filled with guests, among them a Mr. M—— from North Carolina. A storm hit Florida and turned up the coast, and we, with all others on the beach, were advised to leave, as it looked as if the storm would strike us before the next morning.

Mrs. Whaley invited us to spend the night at her home. When we arrived at the plantation, the rain was coming down in torrents, and the wind was blowing so hard that we could feel the car sway as we turned up the long driveway. Just as we entered the large hallway there came a loud popping sound, and we were in total darkness. Somewhere nearby a transformer had burned out, or a tree had fallen across the power line. Our hostess said St. Pierre Creek back of the house was rising rapidly. The tide had not gone out all day, and another with the east wind behind it was coming in. But she felt no fear of the water's reaching the house, for there had never been a time when the tide rose beyond the steps.

As long as I live, the memory of that night will be clearly etched on my mind. My youngest son was with the 11th Airborne Division on Luzon in the Philippines. We knew from the newspapers and the fact that mail was not coming through that some event was pending, and I had scarcely moved from the radio all day. Like hundreds of other mothers whose boys were there, my mind was constantly dwelling on my son, especially since there had been rumors of an airborne landing in Japan, and the Japanese had broadcast the terrible things they would do in retaliation to those

(31)

captured. At times I felt that the suspense was more than I could bear; and the night seemed never ending.

Finally, Mr. M—— arose, and throwing his raincoat around him, said he would go out to the car to see if he could get any war news on the radio. Another hour passed. The wind would almost die down and there would come a sinister stillness, and then with a mighty roar it would rise again. We heard the top of one of the large oaks in front of the house crash to the ground, and as the sound died Mr. M—— came back into the house.

"I'm sorry," he said, "but there was so much static I could not hear any war news. I did hear that the storm just hit Beaufort and is headed towards Edisto, so I came in."

Our hostess made some coffee, and we sat in a group, waiting for we knew not what. After a while Mr. M—— asked casually, "What did the man with the lantern want?"

We all — there were eleven in the room — looked at him in amazement and in a chorus asked, "What man?"

"The one who came up to the house on horseback. He was really in a hurry. I can't imagine what could bring anyone out on a night like this."

Mrs. Whaley came to me and put her hand on my shoulder. "Don't worry," she said "Your boy is safe, and no harm will come to Pine Baron or its occupants from this hurricane."

Then, as we sat in the dim lamplight and listened to the storm slowly blow itself out to sea she told the story of her husband's ancestor, William Whaley, a man so hot tempered and fiery that he was called "Powder Bill." Even as a student at South Carolina College in 1835 he was involved in several duels. After his marriage, his young wife learned that a new affair of honor was impending. Failing to secure his promise to give up the duel, she said that she could not bear the uncertainty of its result and begged him to let her go with him to the place near Charleston where it was to be fought. This the husband would not permit, but he compromised with her by posting couriers with fresh horses at five-mile intervals between Edisto and Charleston so that she might know his fate as soon as possible. The news came, and he was unharmed. Since that time, for more than a century, in times of danger the "Galloping Horseman of Pine Baron" brings the news if all is well.

My husband laughs and says his friend fell asleep and dreamed he saw the horseman. Perhaps so — but I have told it as it happened.

The Seabrooks

WILLIAM SEABROOK owned fifteen hundred slaves, and his cotton lands stretched away acre upon acre. His handsome home, built about 1810, has been known by different names. After the death of his first wife, Mary Ann Mikell, in 1819, Mr. Seabrook married Elizabeth Emma Edings, and the place became known for a time as Edings, but afterwards it was called William Seabrook's house. In later years the plantation was bought by a Northerner, who restored the grounds and house and shortened the name to Seabrook House.

The house is close to the water's edge, with an iron railing bordering the portico and the double front steps. Seabrook had his initials molded across the front of the ironwork, where the steps meet. Between Steamboat Creek and the house was a formal garden with a multitude of walkways bordered with boxwood. Here, on warm afternoons in the early spring and late fall, tea was served, and many a frosted glass of julep sipped. It was one servant's duty to protect and tend the mint bed so that the green pungent leaves would be available winter and summer. Some think Hoban, who designed the White House in Washington, was the architect for Seabrook House; and although there is no proof of this, it could be true. Just before the beginning of the nineteenth century Hoban practiced his profession in Charleston; and Robert Mills, who is credited with drawing plans for the beautiful house on Brooklands plantation, studied under him.

In 1825, Lafayette came to South Carolina while on a tour of the United States. Having made his acquaintance in Charleston, Mr. Seabrook invited him to be his guest on Edisto, and the Islanders were pleased and flattered when the invitation was accepted. In his own steamboat, the planter met the Marquis and his party at the mouth of Rock Creek, where they transferred from the larger boat that had brought them from the city. Here the welcoming committee delayed too long, and the ebbing tide deposited the steamboat on a mudbank before it could reach the Seabrook landing. However, the several hours delay before the incoming tide released the boat were forgotten when the boat arrived at Edisto, and the Seabrook slaves unrolled a scarlet velvet carpet for Lafayette to walk ashore.

Dinner was served to a chosen few. According to tradition, at each end of an elegantly appointed table reposed a large silver tureen of diamond-backed terrapin soup, which drew loud praise from the Marquis and a request for the secret family recipe. Servants brought in huge platters of venison, ham, sea-turtle steaks with finns, turkey with oyster sauce, and vegetables grown on the plantation, including boiled palmetto hearts. Desserts were placed on the table — jellies, pies, syllabub, and custards in tall silver casters.

While the dinner party was waiting in the ballroom for the arrival of other guests, the Reverend William States Lee entered, followed by a nurse carrying in her arms a tiny baby, dressed in a long flowing dress of the finest embroidered linen and lace. It was the infant daughter of the

Seabrooks, and the father placed her in the General's arms. "Will you name her?" he asked.

The Marquis hesitated for not a moment. "We will call her Carolina for the state in which she was born," he replied, "and I will consider it an honor to add Lafayette for myself." So the Reverend Lee christened the child "Carolina Lafayette," and though other names have been carried on in the family from one generation to the next, this name has been reserved for her alone.

II

In the early part of the nineteenth century the planters on Edisto were hard working, practical men, who left it for their children and grandchildren to revel in the luxury brought by the wealth that they had accumulated. Mr. Seabrook was a gentle, lovable man, but he was also an able planter demanding a fair return from his slaves. His holdings grew, and he bought plantation after plantation, always giving his overseers and the plantings his personal supervision. This was probably one of the main reasons for his great success.

Many stories have come down concerning him — simple homely stories. One is told of a trip he made to New York, where the waiter in his hotel asked his preference in drinks. Mr. Seabrook answered "Bring me tea; and be sure it's 'store bought.'" The tea served on his plantation was made from dried leaves of the Cassina berry that grows all over the Island.

Another story illustrates Seabrook's humor. Once, when he was entertaining members of the Agricultural Society, conversation grew into friendly argument, and the men began emphasizing their points in the debate by pounding on the large fragile banquet table. Finally, both argument and table collapsed, when several of the slender square legs were broken. Mr. Seabrook calmly ordered servants to remove the shattered dishes and to bring books from the library to serve as temporary legs. When the task was finished, one book was left over. Mr. Seabrook looked at it with a twinkle in his eyes. "Place the book back on the shelf," he told his servant, "it will be our circulating library until the table is repaired."

When William Seabrook's son by his first marriage returned home after studying a year in France, he talked enthusiastically and endlessly about the wonders of Paris. Finally, becoming a little bored, his father looked indulgently at the young man and lapsing into the Gullah of the Island said, "Yuh like 'um son, I buy 'um fur yuh." With so much money available, the planter's idea of his wealth became a little confused, and the buying of a glamorous French city seemed a minor matter.

III

Years passed. They were full, happy, profitable years for "Uncle Billy," as Mr. Seabrook became known to his kin. But there came a time in 1836 when days would pass without the Islanders seeing his familiar figure riding over his plantations. Mr. Seabrook was feeling poorly, and even the maturing cotton seemed to interest him little. Doctors were called from Charleston, but they gravely shook their heads and gave the family no hope.

September came, the fields were white, and the cotton was ready for picking. Hundreds of slaves sang together as they gathered the snowy bolls into the bags tied across their shoulders. Loud and clear, or sweet and low, the music echoed across the fields and marshes until it reached the "big house," where, unknown to the laborers, a different scene was taking place. Servants tiptoed and whispered, and a hush lay over the mansion. Upstairs, in one of the large bedrooms, William Seabrook lay dying in his wide canopied bed. The dynasty he had helped to found was in its heyday, and its prosperity was to go on for over two decades — until the guns at Fort Sumter blazed forth and started the crumpling of an empire.

Often, men of great wealth pay for their riches by losing the love of their fellow men. With William Seabrook this was not so. Sadly and slowly, for nearly two hours, his funeral procession moved under the widespread oaks that form an avenue in front of his house, across the road that leads to the wharf at Steamboat Landing where thousands of pounds of fine Sea Island cotton were started on their journey overseas. "Formed by sorrowing relatives and friends, masters and slaves, weeping children and solemn dignitaries," the procession came finally to stop in a quiet bower under great trees, and here William Seabrook was laid to rest by the side of his first love.

On the wall of the Edisto Island Presbyterian Church is a marble plaque: "In memory of William Seabrook who departed this life September 1st 1836, aged 63 years, 6 months, 16 days. As a man, he was kind and amiable; as a citizen, enlightened and patriotic. In his social relations, tender, affectionate and unostentationally charitable. In his intercourse with society courteous and conciliatory. As a member of this corporation, active, regular and faithful. As a Christian humble, full of faith and exemplary in his conduct. As an Elder of this church, prudent and zealous. He lived beloved and died lamented by every member of this community. In testimony of their high estimation of his character, the excellence of his example, this monument has been erected by the unanimous consent of the members of this Corporation."

IV

In an atmosphere of fabulous wealth Carolina Lafayette and her half-brother, named William Seabrook for his father, spent their youth.

When the younger William Seabrook and Martha Edings, a sister of William's stepmother, were married in 1828, they built Oak Island, naming it for the fine trees around it. Here they lived in almost unbelievable luxury; and here, shortly before the Confederate War, their son brought his bride. In her unpublished reminiscences written after the war she tells of Oak Island: "I became so accustomed to its grandeur it ceased to impress me. Federal troops landed at the wharf in numbers and came to this elegant old house with its twenty-one completely furnished rooms — lawns encircling the house occupied acres, outbuildings of every description, camellias of every known species, 1500 varieties of roses, an apiary and fish pond in the middle of which there was a latticed house covered with roses. A rustic bridge crossed to the Island. Walkways were covered with crushed shells. At the end of the avenue there was a park with many deer — including a white one. There was a quaint brick house where an iron chest of select wines were kept. Near the water was a dairy, a building made of crushed shells. Just beyond the dairy was a large long boat house. Sail and row boats were kept there and above were the bath houses. In the carriage house were seven or eight vehicles. The family used to ride to Virginia Springs and carriages were kept there during their stay and sent home the first of September when the family went to New York."

Carolina Lafayette grew to be a beautiful woman. She and her sister, Martha Washington Seabrook, visited Lafayette's family in France, where they were presented to Louis Philippe and entertained in the highest court circles. The grace and beauty of the two girls were greatly admired — so much so that before they returned to America Martha was engaged to Lafayette's nephew, Count Ferdinard de Las Teyrie.

Stopping over for a visit in Philadelphia, Carolina met James Hopkinson, a grandson of the signer of the Declaration of Independence from New Jersey, and the young Northerner was so impressed with the Southern girl that he followed her to South Carolina and laid siege to her heart. He also fell in love with Edisto and wanted to live on the Island, but Carolina liked social life in the North, where she was flattered and entertained and many attentions were showered on her. The artist Sully, for whom it was considered a privilege to sit, petitioned Carolina to let him paint her portrait. Although she consented to marry Mr. Hopkinson, the lumber for the house at Cassina Point lay on the high bluff for three years before Carolina agreed for their home to be built.

Cassina Point was inherited by the Hopkinsons' daughter, Julia, who married Murray LaRoche. While much of Mrs. LaRoche's youth was spent in boarding school and in visiting her father's relatives in Philadelphia, Edisto Island was her home, and she was as familiar with the plantation as she was with the social life in the North. Many of these tales were told to me by her. Her personality held one spellbound. As long as she lived, her mind remained as clear as in her youth. Each weekday morning, until a few days before her death, she came to the Island post office for her mail. In a few minutes a crowd would gather around her — relatives, friends, and strangers. No queen ever held court with more dignity and charm. I saw a little book of poems written on Edisto in 1869 by Washington Gailliard Westcoat. Each one was to, or about "Julia." In the picture that he gives of her he describes a beauty and attractiveness that were hers until her death in her ninety-third year. Edisto Island has never been quite the same without her.

All of the three Seabrook houses are visible and easily accessible from the water, and Federal troops took possession of them in 1863. The officers found the big houses ideal for their headquarters. When the families hurriedly refugeed inland, they left most of the slaves and furnishings intact, the smokehouses stored with meat, and the bountiful gardens filled with vegetables. So, for a time, the Federals lived the life of the Old South.

The Mikells

ISAAC JENKINS MIKELL, the son of Ephraim and Providence Jenkins Mikell, built the lovely house known as Peter's Point (derived from Point Saint Pierre) about 1840. The large building stands looking toward St. Helena Sound on a point between two bold tidal creeks. Mr. Mikell's son described the house as having "twelve great rooms with white and colored marble for inside adornment, a spiral stairway, broad brown stone steps and double piazzas." It is on a high foundation of brick and tabby, a construction left as a heritage to the Sea Islanders by the Spaniards and once used widely on the coast. Sea shells, broken and burned, made a lime, which mixed with sand, hardened into a concrete-like substance. Now the making of tabby is a lost art, which vanished along with slaves who practiced it.

The first owner of Point Saint Pierre, during his progress to old age, married four times. Toward the close of his life, a grandchild once said to him, "Grandfather, please tell me about all your wives." The old gentleman replied, "My dear, it has been so long ago I don't remember the first one; the second one was your grandmother, and she brought me wealth and success; the third was the love of my life; and the fourth is the comfort of my old age."

Another family story tells of Mr. Mikell's last marriage. He became interested in a gentle middle-aged lady, one of two sisters, and decided to drive over to her home to ask the important question. On arriving at the house of his intended, he was disappointed to find that she had gone for a visit to Charleston. Nothing daunted, he then asked to see Miss Sara, the sister, and found her so charming and entertaining that he proposed and was accepted.

All the plantations had artificial fishponds. They were considered necessities, and each summer slaves worked steadily to restock them for the winter supply of fish. The pond at Peter's Point was an unusually lovely one, built with an eye for beauty as well as usefulness. Mr. Mikell described it as a "parallelogram, having one of its long sides bricked up on the shore side and a grove of live oaks overshadowing it. The other three sides were dykes reclaiming it from the river, planted with salt-water cedars for beautifying the walks and to protect it from erosion. The pond was of sufficient depth to maintain its briny inhabitants at all stages of the tide. There were several Venetian bridges thrown across to small islands scattered at intervals over its area. On each Island was a diminutive Chinese tea garden."

Mr. Mikell also tells of the slaves and their masters: "An unique feature among us was that we had no poverty. Our slaves, if for no other reason than a business proposition, were well cared for. We enjoyed an abundance of means amounting to riches, and as all were on a social equality, a close scrutiny of one's visiting list was quite unnecessary.

"Our system of agriculture — our only business — was rather feudal in character, in some respects it resembled the system of the old English landowners of an earlier age. The utter indifference to all business outside the plantation was characteristic and seemed a matter of pride to some. To be obliged to attend to business implied restricted means. To many of the older planters the simplest rules of finance seemed to be unknown or ignored. (Factors attended to most business matters.) It is told of one of the wealthiest that when the State Bank of South Carolina was organized in 1802 it allowed its directors to borrow money from it without security. This gentleman in the exercise of his perogative as a director borrowed many thousand dollars. He had absolutely no use for the money and did not take it from the bank. When the time came for settlement, he was exceedingly indignant and protested against the charge of interest, arguing that he had not used the money so he could not see why he should be charged interest."

In his unpublished manuscript, another son of Isaac Jenkins Mikell, Mr. Townsend Mikell, tells of the beginning of the war and afterwards. "I was a student at the University of Virginia when South Carolina withdrew from the Union. I immediately came to Edisto and offered my services to the Governor of the State of South Carolina.

"I joined Calhoun Artillery, made up of Edisto Island men. We served under Major Murray and were stationed at the mouth of the Edisto River. The governor ordered all women, children and disabled men from the Island after the fall of Port Royal. I carried all the family slaves from my father's house, Peter's Point, Bailey's Island, and my brother's Tom's plantation, California, upcountry in to Orangeburg County — some in Sumter and some in Aiken. I came back and joined the South Carolina company of united men until Major Jenkins formed the Rebel Troop.

"I transferred my membership to the Rebel troops under Major Jenkins, who appointed ten scouts to be stationed on Edisto Island to watch for approach of the enemy's gunboats and make daily reports of what transpired in N. Edisto River to General Hagood stationed at Adams Run. The scouts were Townsend Mikell, Alonzo Lee, Robert Seabrook, W. B. Whaley, Joseph Edings, Joe Wescoat, Willie Murray, William Baynard, Dade Wescoat, and Fred Bailey.

"On April 8, 1863, we were captured by a scouting party of the navy. A Negro, James Hutchison, betrayed us. The Scouts were at Arthur Whaley's place; that is, the old Tom Seabrook place, resting and talking over events of the day. My servant, James Giles, was outside in the servants quarters and gave the alarm that the enemy was approaching and then jumped out the back window of the house and ran to the river, plunged in and escaped.

"The Yankees had surrounded the dwelling and captured us. They had come up the river, landed at Middleton's place, and were scouting over the Island. We were put on a boat and carried to Hilton Head.

"After the war Pa and I went to Edisto Island to get our property restored. When we got there we found the house at Peter's Point filled with Negroes — several with small-pox. After getting them to leave we put cloride of lime over everything for a disinfectant. We spent about a month clean-ing up and then went upcountry and brought the family down.

"The Negroes on the place were in a fearful condition — there was much smallpox — they had no work and were de-pendent on oysters, fish, and palmetto cabbage for food. Pa went to Charleston and brought up food of all kinds — bacon, flour, molasses, etc.

"The Negroes were in possession of the Island and or-ganized a military company. They had a great time drilling and marching. We could not know what would be the out-come. All agreed that it was necessary for us to form a com-pany for our own protection. We organized as the 'Mounted Riflemen of Edisto.' Soon afterwards the Negroes disbanded and gave no trouble."

Before leaving the Island in November, 1861, the owner of Peter's Point, like the majority of the Edisto planters, destroyed all plantation crops that could not be moved or hidden. Thousands of dollars worth of fine silky cotton was burned or dumped in the river. Many owners had their Negroes scatter the unginned cotton over the land — any-thing to keep it from benefiting the enemy.

Besides taking numbers of his slaves with him upcountry, Mr. Mikell carried wagons of provisions and farming equip-ment with him. As nearly all farming was done by a laborer with a hoe, the equipment did not take up much room. After arriving at Aiken, Mr. Mikell soon started his Negroes planting a crop to insure food for them and his family. He exchanged large quantities of corn brought from his planta-tion for cloth from the Graniteville Mill. He was evidently a man of foresight and good judgment, for even before he left the Island, he had made plans for his return. His son

(43)

writes: "Father had built on a small island in the swamp, surrounded by water about five feet deep, a large corn crib, holding a thousand bushels of corn, which he filled. This crib was made of green cypress logs and covered with green shingles, entirely noncombustible. He then flatted or lightered over to this island the corn. Afterwards he destroyed the lighter. The crib would not burn and it could not be carted away for the water was too deep. And there it remained to support his people."

After the war, although money was scarce and labor unsatisfactory, the Mikells again successfully planted their land. They went back to the old way of fertilizing with the rich marsh mud that could be had for the taking. As late as 1886 Mr. Townsend Mikell speaks of using this method on his plantation, Sunnyside.

Peter's Point has never been out of the Mikells' possession except during those years between 1861 and 1866. Picturesque and charming, in a setting of palmettoes and huge moss-draped trees, the old house stands serene and stately — a fitting reminder of the generations who have called it home.

The Jenkinses

BRICK HOUSE, ancestral home of the Jenkins family, is thought to have been built in the 1720's by a grandson of Paul Grimball, one of the earliest landowners on Edisto. Paul Hamilton, who became Governor of South Carolina on December 10, 1804, wrote in his journal: "Paul, my father's oldest brother, built a mansion house on Edisto Island (now owned by Joseph Jenkins), the brick of which he imported from Boston in New England (the sand and gravel mixed in the mortar was all brought from Pon Pon river that it might be free from salt), and the timbers of which were all cypress cut from his own lands on Pon Pon River. The inner work was of cedar, and he allowed no wood to be used that had not been housed and seasoned seven years."

Joseph Jenkins, whose mother was Martha Rippon of Fenwick Hall on James Island, first lived at Edisto on a plantation, Mount Field, in the locality called Seaside. He bought Brick House, according to a relative, "because he was tired of the pirates worrying him from the inlet." Old letters say that Mr. Jenkins was a handsome, distinguished man standing six feet four inches in his stocking feet. Prominent in state affairs, he organized a company of volunteers from Edisto Island during the Revolution. His son Joseph Evans Jenkins was a delegate from Edisto in 1860 at the meeting that was held in Columbia for discussion of Secession. As the arguments flew thick and furious, it is told, Colonel Jenkins arose and said: "Gentlemen, if South Carolina does not secede from the Union, Edisto Island will."

On a bright sunshiny morning in January, 1840, Colonel Joseph Evans Jenkins' daughter Martha went down to the public landing, a short distance from Brick House, to meet her father, expected on the steamboat "Silver Star." He had promised to bring her various articles of finery from Charleston, and she impatiently awaited the arrival of the boat. Once each week, either the "Silver Star" or the "Edistow" stopped on its way from Charleston to Savannah, and then again on the return trip. It was quite an event to the Island people, and there was usually a crowd waiting to receive mail and to meet passengers. The planters stood in groups, discussing politics or other interests of the day, while the women, dressed in the latest fashion, sat in their carriages and called greetings to each other.

A mile away a loud whistle sounded, and in a few minutes the steamboat drew up to the landing. Rushing to meet her father as the passengers came ashore, Martha slipped and would have fallen had not a strong hand caught her arm. Startled, she looked up to see a tall young man with clear brown eyes and sandy hair. "You just missed a bad fall," he said; and releasing her, he disappeared into the crowd.

The young man was John Hamilton Cornish, a young teacher and divinity student. Seeking health, he had left his native Michigan, spent a number of years in Connecticut, journeyed to Charleston, and finally come to Edisto. He was made welcome at Sea Cloud, the home of Mikell Seabrook.

In a letter to his family Cornish tells of the Negroes there. "The house servants are clad as well as the generality of people at the North, and the amount of labor they perform is nothing in comparison to that done by a hired girl in the North. There are four wenches to mind the children and wait upon their mistress, the lady's maid, the seamstress, the washer, two active fellows to wait on the table. A cook and a pastry cook making in all ten or twelve. There are three fellows who take care of the horses and garden and another the puppies; there's one wench who minds the turkeys, another the geese and duck, another the hens, besides three or four little Negroes whose arduous task is to keep the fowls out of the garden. The field hands are provided with shoes and two suits of clothes a year and comfortable dwellings; they have their daily tasks to perform, their daily food assigned them. Their tasks occupy them at the fartherest two-thirds of a day. Each has a little plot to cultivate for himself, and most of them have poultry of their own and several pigs."

Cornish received a kindly welcome from the Islanders. Hardly a Sunday passed that he did not accompany a planter home from church to enjoy his hospitality, and Colonel Jenkins was among the first to entertain the stranger. It was a memorable visit for John Cornish.

When he saw Martha Sarah Jenkins he immediately recognized her as the girl he had saved from falling on the day of his arrival. After a bountiful dinner, the family adjourned to the parlor. It was a warm, early spring day, and an open window let in the bright sunlight and the fragrance of flowers. John Cornish thought of the snowbound spring in his faraway Michigan home and felt he would like to live forever in this land where winter fled so soon.

At her father's suggestion, Martha sat down beside a large harp that stood in a corner of the room and played gracefully and well. From his seat near the door John Cornish studied the fair Southern girl carefully, and the daylight was fading before he took his leave. In the months that followed he was a frequent visitor to Brick House, and no one on Edisto was surprised when wedding invitations were received. Once again, the charm of the Island and a beautiful girl had made a conquest.

II

On a beautiful moonlight night in January, 1855, Burwood, the home of General D. F. Jamison (later president of the Secession Convention) was ablaze with lights. In one of the large upstairs rooms Caroline Jamison had nearly finished dressing for her first dance, her excitement shared by the two maids, who oohed and aahed as they slipped each dainty garment over their young Miss's head. "Hurry, Carrie, it's almost eight o'clock," called a voice from the hall. A bevy of pretty girls, overnight guests from Orangeburg, congregated for a moment in the doorway, talking and laughing. Then, with arms around each other, they went down the broad winding stairway.

Caroline took a final glance in the tall mirror between two windows of her bedroom. Slender, almost fragile, the girl was exquisitely lovely. She wore a pale-blue gown with a low-cut neckline; the full skirt, spread over hoops that stood out from her tiny waist, tumbled in billowy folds around satin-clad feet. With a last pat of rice powder, she ran to catch up with her friends.

There had been much discussion among the girls when they learned that young Captain Micah Jenkins would be at the dance. Micah, a nephew of Joseph Evans Jenkins, graduated from The Citadel in 1854, and he and a classmate, Asbury Coward, soon afterwards organized King's Mountain Military Academy at Yorkville. Captain Jenkins had come to Burwood to discuss with General Jamison the advisability of adding an additional two-year course at the academy, and the General had insisted that he attend the festivities.

Captain Jenkins entered the long drawing room at Burwood just as the strains of the first waltz ended. Later, he was to think no sweeter music was ever heard than the tunes played that night on the piano, mouth harp, drum, and guitar, by four Negro servants in homespun suits. The young captain made a striking picture, with the gold braid and brass buttons of his uniform gleaming in the candlelight, and many a feminine heart skipped a beat at the sight of him. But Micah had eyes for only one — the lovely Caroline.

The new academy had been completed when Micah Jenkins brought her as his bride to Yorkville. The large three-story brick building had a wing on each side — one for Captain Coward's family and the other for Micah Jenkins'. The next few years passed quickly for Micah and Caroline. The school was filled to its capacity; they were deeply in love; a son was born to them, and life was perfect.

When the Confederate War began, the school was closed, and Jenkins and Coward entered the army. The friendship between the two men was a rare one, and before they parted they made a verbal agreement that if either survived the conflict, he would educate the children of the other.

Mrs. Jenkins went first to Edisto Island; then, when the Island was evacuated, she refugeed at Midway, near Orangeburg. She lived from day to day for her husband's letters. They are letters of a brave man with high ideals, longing for his wife and children but dedicated to his duty. He tells of his loneliness on return from the infrequent furloughs home, of battles lost and won, of bravery and cowardice, of flattery and chicanery, of suffering and death. These letters show a man's heart and soul bared to the one he called "my best beloved."

In May, 1864, at the age of twenty-eight, General Micah Jenkins was killed in the "Battle of the Wilderness," and a frail young woman, reared in luxury and shielded from every care, found herself a widow with four small sons, a deserted plantation, and thousands of dollars in nearly worthless Confederate bonds and money. Soon after the war ended, she returned to Edisto, to rear her boys and try to build a new life for them.

In 1865, Colonel Coward reopened the military school, and when Micah Jenkins' sons were of proper age they were enrolled. His promise not forgotten, Colonel Coward educated the children of his friend and former partner.

III

On August 13, 1854, a storm raged all day on Edingsville, and by night it had reached hurricane force. The wind made weird sounds as it whistled through the palmettoes, and at times the terrific gale bent the tall trees until their lacy tops almost touched the ground. Streaks of lightning played over the surf, and the houses trembled with each roar of bursting thunder.

In an upstairs room in one of the large houses fronting the ocean, a woman lay near death. It had been a long vigil for the people gathered around her bedside — the anxious husband, the weary physician, and the faithful old Mauma. Out in the hallway, the house servants stood huddled together, their black faces streaked with tears.

Signs of hopelessness were beginning to show on the husband's face, when there came the lusty cry of a new-born baby. It was the voice of little George Washington Seabrook Jenkins, the son of John Jenkins and his wife Marcelline Murray. The baby's cry seemed to arouse the mother — a faint color showed in her face and her pulse became stronger. The old Mauma turned to Mr. Jenkins and with a cry of joy exclaimed, "De tide e turn. See, Massa, lil Mis e live."

When he grew older, Washy, as his family called him, heard many stories of bravery in his family. The War between the States began. His father, Major of the "Rebel Troop" stationed at Adams Run, participated in numerous dangerous engagements with the enemy. His Uncle "Bunch" (General Micah Jenkins) was killed in the war, and the returning soldiers told incident after incident of his fearlessness.

After the war ended, Major Jenkins returned to Edisto and borrowed heavily to plant nearby Fenwick Island in cotton. Like other Edisto Island planters, he had invested every available dollar in Confederate holdings, and this with the loss of his slaves had left him with few assets. He hoped to regain part of his fortune in the Fenwick Island venture. It was an unusually good year for the growth of the cotton. The fertile land produced luxuriant plants filled with bloom, and acre after acre gave promise of a bountiful crop. But one night a horde of caterpillars swept over the island, and in forty-eight hours not a leaf or bloom was left. To this day, the destruction of the cotton is mentioned in the family as "the tragedy of Fenwick Island." Because of this financial disaster, Washy was unable to complete his education at Princeton, as his father and grandfather had done.

The boy grew to love the sea, and spent many happy hours in his small boat, exploring the small uninhabited islands that dot the South Carolina coast between Beaufort and Edisto. On one of these expeditions to a small island, he suddenly heard a strange voice calling for help, and going toward the sound, he found under a large tree a man, lying desperately ill, calling in delirium foreign names and words.

Half-dragging, half-carrying the sick man, Washy succeeded in placing him in the boat. On reaching Beaufort, with the assistance of the townspeople he cared for the sailor until he recovered and was able to work. The man became known as Antoine Santo, but his true name was Agapeto Zabaijainage. He had been a member of a crew who operated a small trading vessel, and when he became ill, his shipmates in fear of cholera had put him ashore. Santo was an experienced pilot, and in a few years owned his own boat.

Washy often said he was born and had spent his youth in sight of the breakers, and it was natural that he, too, should seek a livelihood on the water. With the assistance of his father, he bought an old tugboat and became the youngest captain on the coast. As the years passed, he bought other boats. The sea was in his blood, and he was never satisfied far from it.

In 1893, Captain Jenkins plied his boat, the "Juno," between Charleston, Beaufort, and Savannah. Early in the morning of April 11, he was returning to Beaufort, where he had made his home since 1884. Stopping at what is now the naval station on Parris Island, he learned that a ship was in distress in a storm a few miles out to sea, and he immediately offered to go to the vessel's assistance. When he called for a volunteer crew, the first man to step forward was Captain Antoine Santo.

Soon the crew was completed, and the little tug with its cargo of brave men set out on its mission of mercy. J. C. Carlisle, then Secretary of the United States Treasury, in a letter to Captain Jenkins which accompanied a "gold medal of honor awarded under provisional Acts of Congress," has vividly described what followed. "It appears that in the forenoon of April 11, 1893, the 'Riga,' bound from Havre, France, to Tybee, Georgia, was driven on the north breakers about seven miles off Port Royal, where she soon went to pieces. The pilot boat 'Charleston' was in the vicinity, and her Captain witnessed it, but was powerless to render any assistance in the teeth of the northeast gale then prevailing.

"The storm was of such intensity that navigation was dangerous even on the sheltered waters of the river, and you needed no further proof that you would be in great peril in taking your tug outside.

"Reaching Bay Point at the mouth of the river, you were unable to see any vessel on the breakers but nevertheless proceeded for a considerable distance, when still failing to discover the bark, you concluded that she had got off and therefore put the 'Juno' about and sought harbor. Running along side the British steamship, 'Kingdom,' which had anchored under the lee of Bay Point to escape the storm, you were informed by the Captain who was on the quarter-deck, that he could see the 'Riga' in the breakers and that she was fast going to pieces, her masts having fallen before you cleared the point on your way out.

"Upon this information you once again headed your tug seaward. After passing Fishing Rip buoy the seas broke over the 'Juno,' causing you to fear at each successive plunge that she would never rise again.

"You were about to abandon what seemed a useless struggle when you suddenly made out under the left lee of the north breaker pieces of wreckage with faintly defined forms clinging to them. You pushed the tug forward until you were in the midst of the imperiled men. They were too exhausted to lay hold on the life lines thrown to them, and you placed your crew on your lee side, worked to the windward of the wreckage, and as you came close to the drowning men, your crew reached down and pulled them by the hands on board the 'Juno.' The rescued men were helpless when taken on board and testified if your arrival had been delayed for only a few moments all must have perished.

"Few men can have the privilege of performing an act of such signal service to humanity or possessed of the courage and ability displayed by you under these hazardous circumstances."

Each member of the crew was presented a silver medal similar to the gold one Captain Jenkins received. The rescued sailors drew up resolutions of appreciation, and the King of Norway, from whose country the shipwrecked bark came, sent three beautiful medals to be given "one to Captain Jenkins and the other two to Pilots Antoine Santo and James T. McGrath respectively."

IV

Brick House, like many very old houses in the Low Country, has its ghost stories.

Soon after Joseph Jenkins purchased Brick House, a relative of his wife's came from her home on James Island to visit. The girl Amelia was very beautiful and popular, and her engagement to a member of a prominent Charleston family had just been announced. But shortly after her arrival on Edisto she met a wealthy young planter, and almost instantly they fell in love. When Amelia wrote to her fiancé and asked to be released from the engagement, the gentleman appeared at Brick House and demanded an explanation. On being told she no longer loved him and that she was planning to marry Mr. F——, the jilted suitor pleaded with her to reconsider; and when she refused he said angrily, "You will never marry him. I would rather see you dead." With these words spoken, he walked away.

On the day of wedding, everyone seemed to have forgotten the threat. Mr. Jenkins' private steamboat was waiting at the wharf, almost in sight of Brick House, to take the young couple to Charleston immediately after the wedding. The house was bustling with guests and servants. From the kitchen came tantalizing odors of baking hams, and the pantry shelves were lined with crocks of rich milk ready to be made into syllabub.

In the early evening Amelia went upstairs to dress for her wedding. After Maum Tamer, who had come from James Island with her young mistress, finished arranging the veil and left the room, Amelia heard her name softly called. Going to an open window, she peered into the darkness. Suddenly a shot rang out; then another was heard.

For an instant, a clutch of icy fear held the listeners below spellbound. Then, with one accord, they rushed up the stairs. The bridegroom was the first to reach the girl, but neither he nor anyone else could help her. Her white satin wedding gown stained with blood, she lay dead.

The crimson print of a small hand beside the window showed where the unfortunate girl had tried to steady herself before falling. It is said that it remained there on the beautiful scenic-painted wall until nearly a century later, when it was covered with thick green paint.

The unhappy man who had climbed the big oak that stands opposite the bedroom window turned the pistol on himself; his body was found beneath the tree.

Each year on the night of August the thirteenth, the anniversary of the tragedy, so the legend goes, screams coming from the ancient building can be heard; and, even though the interior of Brick House has been destroyed by fire, some people say that Amelia is often seen at the window — her wedding dress shimmering in the moonlight.

PLATE I: *A reminder of the gracious living that Sea Island cotton brought to Edisto in the years before the Confederate War, Seabrook House, built about 1810, gleams in the sunlight beyond live oaks and gray Spanish moss. Here Lafayette visited in 1825 and at William Seabrook's request named the planter's daughter—"Carolina Lafayette." The home is now owned by Mr. and Mrs. D. D. Dodge of Philadelphia.*

PLATE II: *Cassina Point was the home of Carolina La-fayette Seabrook and James Hopkinson, the young North-erner, who fell in love with her and Edisto Island as well. It is said that Carolina preferred social life at the North and that the lumber for the house lay on the spot chosen for their home for three years before she consented to have it built. Cassina Point is owned by Mr. and Mrs. LaRoche Seabrook.*

PLATE III: *The present Episcopal Church building is the third in which Edisto Islanders have worshipped. The first church was replaced by a new building in 1840; and the second building, having survived the Confederate War, during which it was used by both armies, was destroyed by fire in 1876.*

PLATE IV: *Seaside, now the home of Admiral and Mrs. C. D. Murphey, was once called Locksley Hall and as such was known as a "house of tragedy." Two suicides, two accidental deaths, a probable murder, and a persistent ghost accounted for its former reputation, which has now disappeared with its old name.*

PLATE V: *"In the name of God and by the authority of the United States Government, we are here to reclaim our church!" proclaimed the Reverend William States Lee after the Confederate War to the astonished Freedmen who had taken over the Presbyterian Church while its regular congregation had refugeed Up Country during the Federal occupation. Built in the 1830's, the church is considered one of the most beautiful in the Carolina Low Country.*

PLATE VI: *The Presbyterian Parsonage on Edisto. Henry Bowers' grant of land for the support of a Presbyterian minister in 1717 marks the beginning of the "oldest uninterrupted Presbyterian organization in South Carolina." Earlier records were destroyed during the Revolutionary War, but the Session Minute Book provides a continuous history of the years since 1790.*

PLATE VII: *Once the home of a branch of the Whaley family, Windsor, located on Russel Creek, is now owned by Mrs. N. A. Anderson of Charleston. The last member of the Whaley family to live at Windsor "never gave up hope that the famous Sea Island cotton would again bring prosperity back to Edisto Island, and as long as he lived he planted a small patch of seed cotton."*

PLATE VIII: *Sunnyside, built by Townsend Mikell shortly after the Confederate War, is adorned with a cupola, reminiscent of Bleak Hall, the Townsend ancestral home where Mr. Mikell was born. The cannon in front, possibly a pirate gun dating from before the Revolution, was found by Mr. Mikell's servants, while they were digging gravel for the making of "tabby." Sunnyside is the summer home of Mr. and Mrs. Edwin Belser of Columbia, S.C.*

PLATE IX: *Middleton, the home of the Pope family for many years, was once known as Chisolm House. Here Mrs. Robert Chisolm defied the church officer who told her that her dead husband could not rest in hallowed ground, and from here she started on her errand that made removal of his body impossible.*

PLATE X: *Old House, formerly called Four Chimneys, owned by Mr. and Mrs. Arthur F. Langley, was once owned by the Whaley family. The Palladian door, the fanlight, and Doric columns show the influence of the classical revival on even comparatively simple homes.*

PLATE XI: *"The ancient houses stand proudly—some in garbs of glistening white; others seemingly dressed in deepest mourning, with sagging porches and weathered walls. . . ." Brooklands, credited to the design of Robert Mills, is owned by Captain Teddy Bailey.*

PLATE XII: *Built in 1790 for Ephraim Baynard, Prospect Hill had doors of solid mahogany and doorknobs of silver. Once pursued all the way from the Presbyterian churchyard to Prospect Hill by a "ghost," Baynard himself, years after his death, disturbed the rest of a Negro retainer who slept in one of the basement rooms. The house is now owned by P. H. Whaley of Washington, D.C.*

PLATE XIII: *Peter's Point, or Point St. Pierre, with a lovely double piazza and a foundation of brick and tabby, was built for Isaac Jenkins Mikell about 1840. The house has "twelve great rooms with white and colored marble for inside adornment."*

PLATE XIV: *The last remaining slave houses at Cassina Point (Plate II). Note the similarity in construction of these cabins in the "row" and that of the "big house." Like their master, the servants lived in houses with clapboard sidings, pitched roofs, and ornamental chimneys.*

PLATE XV: *Two orange trees, filled with fruit, grow beside the ruins of Brick House, built in the 1720's by Paul Hamilton of brick imported from New England. Here, over a hundred years later, the young Northerner John Cornish wooed and won Martha Jenkins, whose family had acquired the home in 1798.*

PLATE XVI: *As Edisto's planters prospered with Sea Island cotton, they built impressive town houses in Charleston, where they resided for the social season. Isaac Jenkins Mikell's home in the city, now occupied by the Charleston Free Library, is a fine example of the classical revival of the 1850's.*

Other Families and Their Homes

PROSPECT HILL, designed by James Hoban, was built for Ephraim Baynard in 1790. The doorknobs were of silver, and the large thick doors of solid mahogany. Unlike most of the big houses on Edisto, the basement at Prospect Hill is enclosed, and the space used for storage, kitchen, and dining room.

Mr. Baynard was very rich, and his stables of high stepping thoroughbred horses were famous. It is a tradition that at night when the wind is high, persons in the house can hear the sound of wheels, the crack of a whip, and the beat of horses' hooves sweeping up the steep driveway and around the house, to stop abruptly at the front door. The sister of the present owner of the house told me she had often heard the sound; she thought that the way the wind blows through the palmettoes produces the illusion.

Soon after Mrs. R——'s brother bought Prospect Hill, the aged Negro who had been caretaker on the plantation for many years said that he had often been bothered by the ghosts of the original owners. Whenever old Henry slept in a small room in the basement, Mrs. Baynard walked up the stairs from the wine closet, always rattling a bunch of keys, and Mr. Baynard kept knocking on the door and calling in a loud voice. When the new owner inquired if "sparits" were still annoying him, the caretaker replied, "That ole man worry me too much, but other night I jist tole him, 'Mr. Baynard,' I says, 'it ain't no use for youse to come worry me fur yuh ain't own dis place no more.' And I ain't seen um since, suh."

Another story tells how Ephraim Baynard himself had an encounter with a ghost. Having ridden a favorite horse to the public landing to meet a boat bringing him merchandise from Charleston, he fastened the packages securely to his saddle and started for home, but on passing near the avenue leading to a friend's house, he decided to stop for a visit. Several hours and toddies later, he again mounted his horse, flicked the whip, and was soon on the highway. By the time he reached the Presbyterian churchyard it was quite dark. A sudden gust of wind and a jerk on his saddle caused him to look around. A great billowy white mass seemed to be following him. He dug his spurs into the flanks of the sensitive horse, and it quickened its pace. But soon Ephraim Baynard felt another tug, and a backward glance showed him that the huge mass was almost upon him. Again he spurred, and the horse seemed to move on wings. When Mr. Baynard reached home and the servant ran to take his mount, the rider fell to the ground, for the gallant animal was dead beneath him. Stretched behind the horse was a long cloth of fine white linen that had come on the boat and worked loose from the bundle during the ride.

II

Adjoining Prospect Hill is Meggett's Point, once the home of the Meggetts, the Clarks, and the Murrays. At the time of the Confederate War it was owned by Dr. Joseph J. Murray. Later it was bought by the Griffens, seafaring folk who came down from the East.

In the same locality stands stately Brooklands, whose beautiful lines are credited to the designing of Robert Mills. It is owned by Captain Teddy Bailey. The old graveyard near the house testifies that the Seabrooks and Jenkinses at one time lived there. A short distance away was the home of Dr. William Bailey. It was built in the shape of a Maltese cross. Another Bailey home, Laurel Hill, stood nearby. Near the highway is Frogmore, the home of Colonel Arthur Bailey.

Bordering the main highway one can see the broad fertile fields of the old Hanahan Plantation, now called "Henions" by the Negroes. It was also at one time the seat of a member of the Whaley family. It is easy to picture the level fields white with cotton. The old house was burned, but it stood on a beautiful site on the bank of the South Edisto River looking towards Johossee Island.

There is Gun Bluff, the plantation of Governor Whitemarsh Seabrook, who lies buried there. Some say Governor Morton's grave is on the Island, but I have been unable to find it.

The Presbyterian parsonage is a fine example of the Sea Island houses. It was built about 1840 for the Reverend William States Lee, who was pastor of the church for over fifty years. The tall two-story house faces a tidal creek; it stands high off the ground on a tabby foundation, and there is a wide piazza across the front. Before the War the church furnished the pastor with a house and forty acres of land in addition to his salary. Records show that Mr. Lee owned a number of slaves and lived in a manner comparable to that of his wealthy congregation. He was greatly beloved on the Island.

III

Chisolm House was built by Dr. Robert Chisolm for his wife Mary Edings. It is a large square house with two wings and a broad piazza. It later became known as Middleton. The owner, suffering from an incurable disease and intense pain, committed suicide and was buried in one of the churchyards. Later an officer of the church gently told Mrs. Chisolm "that it was contrary to the custom and law of the church to allow any suicide to be buried in that hallowed spot" and that as a representative of the church he was forced to ask her to remove the body.

Without answering her caller, the bereft woman left the room weeping bitterly, but immediately she gave orders for her largest boat to be made ready for a trip to Charleston. With twelve oarsmen she made the journey and returned home with her purchases. In the silence of the night she had a wall placed around her beloved's grave and defied anyone to touch it. And no one dared; today she rests by his side. Middleton has belonged to the Popes for many years.

Nearby is Cypress Trees, the home of the Murrays. Dr. J. J. Murray, brother of Mrs. Marcelline Murray Jenkins, was a well-known beloved physician. One incident gives an indication of the esteem in which he was held. Near the end of the war, Dr. Murray's horse was shot beneath him, but fortunately he was not injured. Immediately there was a petition circulated to replace it, and seventy-eight names, the number necessary for the purchase, were signed in a few minutes; and this was at a time when pay was slow and Confederate money worth little. Another Murray plantation is on the Island, just across the creek from Edingsville.

The Wescoats' big house and the beautiful Episcopal Church (which was said to be a minature St. Michael's) were destroyed when fire from a burning field got out of control.

Across the creek from the site of the Wescoat house is Sunnyside, the plantation home of the late Townsend Mikell. At the time of his death he was the oldest elder in the Presbyterian church. Sunnyside is on a little island in St. Pierre Creek. The late Mr. Tom Mikell's plantation, California, on the Peter's Point road, is now a part of Sunnyside plantation.

On towards the ocean, on "The Neck," there stood a house once occupied by some members of the Edings family, and Whaleys also once lived there. The first time I saw the house a lovely Winthrop desk stood on the sagging porch, but the wind was banging the solid wooden shutters against paneless windows. Empty and isolated, the house lost its doors and fine carved interior to vandals; gales and tides gradually took the rest, and now nothing of the fine old home remains.

IV

Locksley Hall is one of the oldest houses on the Island. It is thought to have been built for William Edings before the Revolution. So much sorrow has occurred within its walls that it could well be called the "house of tragedy." Two small Edings children were stricken by diphtheria and died there. One of the owners cut his throat and bled to death; and it is told that, although over a century has passed since his death, no amount of sanding, paint, or varnish can hide the bloodstains on the floor, and at night one can hear the drip, drip of blood as it falls to the dining room beneath the room where the suicide took place.

Then, there is the story of the boy, a close relative of the Edingses, who was left an orphan and went to live at Locksley Hall. When he was seventeen years of age he returned from a hunting trip; and as he went up the stairs he met his old Mauma, who had been with him since he was born. The young man handed her his gun, and it accidently discharged and killed the woman. Grief-stricken, the boy picked up the gun and shot himself.

The house was occupied for a time after the War by carpetbaggers named Wright. Later a family of McConkies bought it, and the elegant name Locksley Hall gave way to the name "McConkies." During the residence of the McConkies a sister was burned to death and a brother was found dead in the stable. It was reported that he was kicked by a mule, but it was generally thought that he was murdered and placed in the stable after being robbed of the large sum of money he always carried.

For a time tenants lived in the house, and then it was acquired by one of the old Islanders. The trail of tragedy had not ended, for this owner was badly injured in an automobile accident and never recovered from the effects of it.

The house was bought a few years ago by a retired naval officer, and he and his charming wife are bringing it back to its former beauty. Now it is felt that a new era has dawned for the old place and the shadows of the past have been forever lifted.

The Stevenses lived by Store Creek, which flows out of St. Pierre. It is supposedly called that because for years a store has been kept near the creek. On ancient maps it appears as Palmeter Creek, and several plats of land bordering it bear that name.

Old deeds, church records, and histories mention such families as Fripp, McLeod, Russel, Lardant, Bower, Whippy, Fickling, Calder, and numbers of others, but I could not find anything about them.

The planters on Edisto Island probably owned more slaves than could be found in any other place of its size, and in all the time I have spent on the Island I've heard only one story of cruelty to a slave. The owner was severely censured by his neighbors, and he was either so penitent or ashamed it never happened again. It was in the summer of 1832 — so the story goes — and the Negro's owner was on Edingsville. Becoming angry with the slave for some misdemeanor, he ordered the Negro bound in a crouching position to the back of a high-wheeled racing cart. He then ordered six slaves to pull the cart to his plantation about fifteen miles away, as an example to others who might be tempted to be disobedient. It is told that in his old age the planter was afflicted with rheumatism and drawn in exactly the same crouching position in which the slave was held.

One often-told story illustrates how the Island's planters thought of themselves and their surroundings. One day, after his afternoon nap a planter, dressed in fine broadcloth and imported linen vestcoat, came down his stairway and ordered his steamboat readied for a trip. Just that morning, he had told his wife, he had received a letter from Charleston informing him of the imprisonment of Napoleon on St. Helena Island, and he was going across the river to call on him.

There were other old plantations on the Island — among them Shell House, Cedar Hall, and Ravenswood; but they, like the people who lived there, have disappeared into the past.

The Negroes

Children of the King

ACCORDING to tradition, many of the Negroes on Edisto are descended from an African king brought captive to the Island during the early days of slave trading. They are coal-black, tall, straight, and well formed. The women's hands are slender, and their fingers taper to long oval nails that no amount of hard work seems to blunt or disfigure. There probably is less mixed blood among the Negroes here than anywhere else in America. A mulatto is rarely seen, and even today it is seldom that one of the Negroes marries outside his clan. Their happy dispositions and contentment show plainly in their faces. They are loyal, generous, rich in humor, and wise in sizing up a stranger.

After a glance an Edisto Island Negro can place you. He knows only two classes — poor buckra and quality. Poor buckra means something more intangible than lack of worldly goods; in fact, many of the ones so designated are numbered among the "new rich." Only dire necessity will cause an old Edisto Island Negro to work for "sich."

I went to see Josephine Wright, who has lived on the Island all of her life and is so old she remembers when the "last big gun shoot" in 1865. After talking with her for nearly an hour, I gave her a small present as I started out the door. She thanked me profusely and said: "Yunnah wait Missus." Going to an old sideboard she removed a clean white cloth from over a box containing three eggs. Handing me two of them, she graciously said, "Yunnah tak de aigs."

I commented on some old pressed-glass goblets and a little pitcher on the sideboard, and Josephine told me they had belonged to her mother. I feel sure that Josephine's children will place them on her grave when she dies. Sometimes one sees on the graves pieces of old colored glassware and copper luster that would make a collector pause and look longingly.

There are at least twelve Negro churches on Edisto Island — Presbyterian, Methodist, Episcopalian, and Baptist. The women of the churches keep them spotlessly clean. Many of the altars are covered with lace curtains, and crocheted "tidies" decorate the back of chairs in the pulpit.

The Gullah spoken by the Edisto Island Negroes is not a written language, and there are no words to describe it; the soft voices can give it the sound of sweetest music or the guttural rumbling of a distant storm. To a person hearing it for the first time it is a foreign tongue, especially if it is spoken rapidly. Even after years of hearing it daily for months at a time, I cannot understand it easily.

A story is told that during World War II, when the Japanese were intercepting our code messages, an officer hearing one of the Edisto Island Negroes speak decided to teach him to broadcast to our armed forces. To the amazement of the Japanese there was not a person among them who could decipher the new "code." I do not know if the story is true, but it is perfectly plausible.

After the Confederate War the Negroes bought tax-land from the United States Government. Some of them built close together and called the settlement Freedsman Village. Others chose sites nearer the creeks. Many of these houses are still occupied, although the roofs leak and often the walls are propped up with long poles. Instead of a chimney, a stove pipe protrudes a foot or so from one side of the house. The old houses have no screens; and, although it was once supposed the Negroes were immune to mosquitoes, on hot summer nights when the wind is still the odor of old automobile tires and rags burning is thick in the air.

Nearly all the older people own their homes, but it would take a multitude of lawyers to untangle the titles. The property has passed from parents to children for eighty-nine years, and the legal owners are scattered all over the country. There has been no division, and in many instances the titles are still in the names of the original purchasers. One member of the family remains at home, and during vacation the others feel free to visit. They come from Michigan, New Jersey, and New York, dressed in city clothes and driving their own shiny new cars. The tiny houses overflow with children and grandchildren. When a baby is born to a straying daughter, she usually goes to the nearby city to work, and the grandmother raises the child along with her own younger ones. The tie of blood is strong, and no child ever goes so far on the downward path that loving words and shelter are denied him.

"Honey in duh Rock"

MUSIC and religion have always played an important part in the lives of the Negroes of Edisto and all along the Carolina coast. Their songs, mostly spirituals, are sung in their churches, in the fields, and under the trees where they gather on warm days. At first dark, the singers come from all directions — singly and sometimes in groups of a dozen or more. I have seen as many as a hundred at one place.

The music rings out sweet and clear. It has an unearthly sound, and you listen breathlessly, half-expecting to hear the rustle of angel wings. The songs have been handed down orally for generations, with new stanzas added from time to time. Plantations and localities have their own songs, and variations of songs. One that is sung by the Negroes on all the Sea Islands is "Who Buil' the Aak"; but probably the best known of the Edisto plantation spirituals is "Lookin' Down Dat Lonesome Road." It is sung with much pathos and handclapping.

Another of the old spirituals is "Honey in duh Rock." I went to see six of the oldest colored people on Edisto before I was able to find anyone who remembered it. One, a colored minister, who had passed his ninety-first birthday said, "Missus, I'se got dat song on muh mouth but I jist cannuh remember it."

Honey in duh rock
Fur to feed God's chillun
Feed every chile of Grace
Honey in duh rock
Honey in duh rock
Fur to feed God's chillun
Feed every chile of Grace

Oh Love in duh rock
Fur to feed God's chillun
Feed every chile of Grace
Love in duh rock
Love in duh rock
Fur to feed God's chillun
Feed every chile of Grace

Faith in duh rock
Fur to feed God's chillun
Feed every chile of Grace
Faith in duh rock
Faith in duh rock
Fur to feed God's chillun
Feed every chile of Grace

It is almost impossible to get the words to many of the songs because they are "make-up songs," improvised each time they are sung.

Two of the very oldest spirituals are "Limpin' Jedus" and "Angel Roll duh Stone Away." As far as I know, they have never before been printed. One of the old-timers said, when asked if he remembered them, "I knows um en muh head, but I can't rightly put muh tongue to um. Muh mudder sing um en de rebel time."

Andrena, who lives near the Burrough, after much prompting and prodding by others, sang "Limpin' Jedus." ("See-me" is run together and sounds like "Sim-mee.")

> See-me, Oh see-me, see-me
> Oh Limpin' Jedus see-me, see-me here
> Goin' to heaven see-me
> Oh Limpin' Jedus see-me, see-me
> Oh Lawd I'm goin' to heaven
> See-me, see-me home.
>
> Up on the mountain see-me, see-me
> Oh Limpin' Jedus see-me, see-me here
> Goin' to heaven see-me, see-me
> Oh Limpin' Jedus see-me, see-me
> Oh Lawd I'm goin' to heaven
> See-me, see-me home.
>
> Down in the valley see-me, see-me
> Oh Limpin' Jedus see-me, see-me here
> Goin' to heaven see-me, see-me
> Oh Limpin' Jedus see-me, see-me
> Oh Lawd I'm goin' to heaven
> See-me, see-me home.

Carrie Smith, who lives in Seaside, sang it differently:

> I'm reelin' an rockin'
> Sometimes I'm up
> Sometimes I'm down
> Oh Limpin' Jedus see-me
> See-me, see-me here.

I'm on my way to heaven, Lord
See-me, see-me here
Through all my trials and crosses
See-me, see-me here
Oh Limpin' Jedus see-me home.

Molly Gadston was the only one who remembered any of
the words to "Angel Roll duh Stone Away."

Angel roll duh stone away
Angel roll duh stone away
On a bright new Sunday mornin'
Angel roll duh stone away.

Yonder come little angel
Comin' by duh breakin' of duh day
Bring good news from heaven
Oh Angel roll duh stone away.

Angel roll duh stone away
Angel roll duh stone away
On a bright new Sunday mornin'
She roll duh stone away.

"Didn't it Rain?" once was sung in all the praise houses:

Didn't it rain my chillun, rain oh my Lord
Didn't, oh didn't it, oh didn't it
Oh my Lord, didn't it rain.

It rained forty days and it rained forty nights
There wasn't no land nowhere in sight;
God sent a raven to bring the news,
He hoist his wings and away he flew,

To the East, to the West, to the North, to the South
All day, all night, oh, tell me didn't it rain,
    chillun, rain
Oh my Lord didn't it rain.

It rained forth days, forty nights without stoppin'
Noah wus glad when duh rain stopped droppin';
When I git to Heaven goin' put on my shoes
En walk aroun' Heaven an tell duh news.

How it rained in the east, how it rained in the west;
All day, all night, listen to duh rain
Didn't it rain chillun rain
Oh my Lord, didn't it, didn't it, oh didn't it
Oh my Lord didn't it rain.

A knock at the window, a knock at the door;
They cried "Oh Noah, please take me in"
But Noah cried out that "You're full of sin,
My Lord's got the key, you can't get in."

Just listen to the rain, in the North, in the South
In the east, in the west,
Didn't it rain.

One Sunday morning in September, near one of the tidal
creeks, we saw a baptism in progress. Before the eyes of
about one hundred and fifty spectators, the candidate, the
leader, and the preacher stood waist-deep in the water. All
three were dressed in white flowing shroud-like robes, and
they wore turbans. The candidate was dipped three times in
the ebbing tide (the Negroes believe it carries their sins
away). Then wrapped in a quilt, she was hurried shivering
up the highway to the church about one hundred yards away.
A sister walked on each side of her. As we drove away, the
words of the baptismal-communion hymn came softly from
the church:

When I fall upon my knees and I face the rising sun
Oh Lord have mercy on me, Oh Lord have mercy on me
We're goin' to break the bread together on our knees
We're goin' to break the bread together on our knees

Yes, we're goin' to drink the wine together on our knees
Yes, we're goin' to drink the wine together on our knees
When I fall upon my knees and I face the rising sun
Oh Lord have mercy one me, Oh Lord have mercy on me.

The Negroes attend their churches faithfully. In the last
decade many of the members have gone to faraway cities to
live, but when death occurs they are brought home, where
services are conducted in the church of their childhood, and
they are laid to rest in their native soil. Monuments are
erected in accordance with the family's prosperity.

On Sundays, from early morning to late afternoon, the
road is bright with gay colors. The churchgoers can be seen
singly or in groups. Girls walk together, with young bucks
following; or, more often, boys and girls walk side by
side — sometimes hand in hand. Here and there an old
woman moves slowly, her long black veil trailing, and her
eyes, wise with years of living, gaze with tolerance on her
"grands." Perhaps she is living over another day when her
own steps could keep pace with the swiftly moving ones
ahead. Some of the older men, withered and lean like the
animals they ride, come on horseback. Today a fair number
of cars line the highway in front of a church where a meeting is being held. Some of the radiator caps are decorated
with coon tails, and some with little whirligigs that turn
when the car is in motion.

Feuds can break up a congregation, but usually they are
patched up. Last year a committee from one of the churches
placed a building fund in the custody of the preacher and a
deacon. Time passed, and the new church was not started.
On Sundays small groups began to gather, and whispering
conversations took place. Finally, one more aggressive than
the rest arose in meeting and asked, "W'enebbuh duh buil'in
e started?"

There were evasive answers from the preacher. As the members grew more insistent, the deacon blamed the preacher, and he, eager to escape the wrath of the congregation, blamed the deacon. Soon the church was completely divided. Many refused to attend services, and the few who remained went in a half-hearted, questioning way. The preacher was asked to resign. He refused. The deacon went to another church. The feud is still unsettled. The loyal ones remain, and a few of the straying ones have come back, but the preacher looks out over rows of empty benches.

"The Sanctify"

AT THE TURN of the century, a woman named Tyra Wright bought an old store building and had it torn down and rebuilt in a thicket of pines on Steamboat Road. Tyra was the Priestess, or Church Mother, of a group of Negroes who called themselves "The Sanctify." On meeting days, when darkness fell over the Island, dusky forms could be seen emerging, not from the plantations roads bordered by the sweet-scented tea olives and glossy-leafed magnolias, but from the foot paths trailing out of the dense growths of cassina and myrtle. Through swamps alive with mosquitoes and the deadly diamond-back rattler, they came to worship.

An eyewitness described a service years ago:

"The resonant boom-boom-boom of the tom-toms, the same mystic gripping rhythm that rolled down the Congo long before white men went to the jungles for slaves, still tells a story in the Low Country that the faithful of a Negro tribe are at worship. Their rites are as weird to the casual observer as the swirling dances of their forefathers when the drum beats meant war or worship along the Congo.

"The Sanctify folks always welcome dawn with a blast from a horn and at high noon each day a drum beat — deep, sonorous tum-tum-tum is sounded. At the service witnessed, the Church Mother (the Priestess), an Acolyte and minister were present. Two little Negro boys, their faces alive with smiles, danced. The little fellows danced until they were exhausted and then sat down beside their mothers. The tom-toms were silent.

"The Acolyte read the Scriptures. The faithful testified, each in jerky sentences, the drums started — they rolled slowly at first, then faster until the crashing tum-tum-tums seemed to run together in one long, bewitching beat. The women danced, the little girls seized tambourines. Women swayed and kept time with hand claps. Feet rose and fell in uncanny rhythm. The Priestess was dressed in a man's coat and wore a turban. She danced in her corner — swaying at first, her movements became jerky as the drums poured out constant boom-boom-boom that made muscles twitch. Feet pounded the floor with dull thuds, but each beat was in perfect rhythm. The Priestess raised her voice in high praise and danced like mad. At last the Preacher, or deacon as he calls himself, signalled that the drums cease, but the Priestess continued to whirl and whirl before the altar. The other participants sank to their seats, but the Priestess danced faster and faster. Her face convulsed and her arms jerked. She threw herself on a bench and chanted praises to Heaven. When a woman handed her a tiny baby the spell was broken and the wild rites closed."

The flickering light of the old lanterns no longer cast their shadows over the slender, frail figure of Tyra Wright. When she died, her followers buried her back of the little church she loved, and one has to look closely to find her grave. With her death in 1942 much of the enthusiasm waned, and although a new Church Mother succeeded Tyra

Wright, the meetings have almost ceased. A few of the members still live on Edisto, and they speak reverently of Tyra, but it is almost impossible to persuade them to talk of the services. Occasionally a minister from the City, as Charleston is called, holds a noonday meeting, but with little of the old rituals.

"Revival Pon Top Edisto"

A GOOD story is worth repeating — especially one by a master teller of tales. Nearly half a century ago John Bennett published in the *Southern Review* a story called "Revival Pon Top Edisto." He has graciously consented to let it be reprinted here:

Shortly after the historic earthquake on the coast of South Carolina, the Rev. Isaiah Brown, colored, met the Rev. Oddie Capers, uncolored.

"Good mornin', Misto Capers, suh," says he, "I hope I sees you well!"

"I thank God for health," replied Mr. Capers. "But where have you been this while?"

"Pon top Edisto Islant, conductin' a rebibal. I ain't conduc' 'um bery long, ner I ain't conduc' 'um bery well, and w'en I lef', de rebibal was a-conductin' ob itself!"

"Automatic, eh?"

"No, suh, Southe'n Methodis'. You see, Misto Capers, hit was dishaway: De Rebrin Moses Whaley, w'ut belongs 'pon Edisto, was a-conductin' dis rebibal, an' somehow, hit ain't a-progressin' fuh ter satisfy his mind. Hit ain't gwine his way, hit ain't gwine de Lo'd's way, and, one way nurrah, t'ing ain't gwine de way dey should.

"So he 'peal ter me fuh to come down an' he'p him, couse he knowed my fo'te was prayeh. Sezzee: 'Hit need a man kin pray mo' stronger dan I kin. Come down an' he'p us, do Buh Brown . . de Debble is got Edisto!'

"I gone. Buh Whaley, he meet me at de station, an' he say, sezzee, 'Buh Brown, I dunno w'ut de matteh. I does read de scripcheh ter 'em; I does preach ter 'em; I does pray ter 'em; I does 'xhort wid 'em; we sings de old songs; dey shout, dey clap, dey stomp; but dey ain't come ter de mou'neh's bench . . . an' de Debble is got Edisto!'

" 'Um — Hmm — ' sez I. 'Come along, Buh Whaley, le's we go ter de meetin' an' see w'ut we kin do!'

"We gone ter de meetin'. De chu'ch plum full ter de cornder an' de do'.

"So Buh Whaley tek de Scripcheh, an' he read ter 'um, an' he preach ter 'um, an' he pray wid 'um an' he 'xhort wid 'um. Dey sings de old songs; dey shout, dey clap, dey stomp, but dey ain't come ter de mou'neh's bench . . . an' de Debble is sho' got Edisto!

"Buh Whaley 'zaust himself. Nen he say ter me, sezzee, 'Now, Buh Brown, you try! . . . De meetin' is wid you!'

"So I tek de scripcheh, an' I reads ter 'um, an' I preach ter 'um, an' I 'xhort 'um. We sings de old songs; dey shout; dey clap; dey stomp, but dey ain't come to de mou'neh's bench . . . an' de Debble is sho' 'nuff got Edisto!

"Nen Buh Whaley say ter me: 'W'ut we gwine do, you an' me an' God? We is come ter a stan'still!

"But 'Wait' says I, 'Buh Whaley, wait 'pon de Lo'd, an' be o' good cheer, an' he gwine stren'then you heaht!'

"An' den, Misto Capers, suh, I biggin fuh pray! An' I says 'Oh, Lo'd! Sen' yo' lightnin'! Oh, Lo'd, sen' yo' t'undah! Rouse dese dusty bones!'

"I look out de windoh, Misto Capers, I ain't see no lightin', an' I hain't heah no t'undah! So I tek nurrah round, an' sez I: 'Oh, Lo'd! Oh, Lo'd; Tek dis people . . . tek 'um, Lo'd, an' shek 'um! Tek 'um by de back er deir neck an' shek de gizzard outen' 'um!'

"Des' bout dat time I heah sumpin' go; 'Br-r-r-r-r-roo!' De chu'ch biggin fuh shek! De flatform o' de pulpit trimble! An' sump'n deep down een de belly o' de yuth do 'Burr-rr-rr-rr-rr-rr-oom!' . . . dem chu'ch walls rock an' reel like dey gwine fall!

"Wid dat, all dem people come a-climbin' ober one nurrah, scramblin' ter de mou'neh's bench! . . . Buh Whaley, he gone out *dis* winduh . . . an' I gone out *dat* winduh! An' time I gone out de winduh, sez I: 'Lo'd, de meetin' is wid You!' An' w'ut I says ter you, Misto Capers, suh, it dis: 'Dere ain't no man, w'ite ner black, oughter pray fer w'ut he can't stan' up ter!' "

"Jist a 'ittle"

EDISTO ISLAND has a justified reputation for fine food. The Negroes are instinctively good cooks, and they have followed prized family recipes handed down in the planters' families for generations.

Some years ago, there appeared in *The Baltimore Sun* an article from the *Japan Advertiser* — an example of how far Edisto's reputation has spread.

"The recent celebration of the 250th Anniversary of the settling of Charleston offered an opportunity for the first families of the charming old Carolina City to vie with each other in setting forth tempting dishes to the visitors that thronged the town.

(107)

"Prominent on the menu was the Soup a la Seabrook, and it is to be found in an old cook book carefully written in faded ink. The directions for making it are simple. A large soup bone is dropped into a huge kettle — originally, it hung over the great fireplace in the 'cooking house' on the Seabrook plantation on Edisto. The bone is augmented by large cubes of tenderloin of beef, sliced turnip, okra, tomatoes, potatoes (either white or sweet), beans, green peppers, onions and a few slices of salt pork. These ingredients are covered with cold water and lid fit tightly on the pot, the contents being allowed to simmer two hours or more. As it cooks, plenty of salt, pepper and a dash of sugar are dropped into the kettle, for all Southern food and particularly Carolinian food is highly seasoned.

"Next in importance comes Shrimp a la Creole — a favorite recipe of the Whaley family. Two or three slices of bacon are dropped in a hot saucepan and fried to a crisp. While the bacon is browning, finely chopped Spanish onions are stirred in with the fat meat and likewise browned. Then are added two or three tomatoes cut in cubes. If fresh ones cannot be had a can of tomatoes will do as well. In the mixture is dropped a red pepper. When the tomatoes have cooked to a sauce, carefully washed and peeled fresh shrimp are dropped in the pan and the whole highly seasoned.

"Another dish — Whaley Baked Oysters a la Baynard — is prepared by taking a deep baking dish, first putting in a layer of crisp pastry in the form of tiny biscuits which have previously been baked to a flaky crispness. The layers of oysters and pastry are alternated until the dish is filled. Salt, pepper, and lumps of butter are sprinkled throughout the layers, the whole being covered with enough milk to keep from burning, whisked into a hot oven and baked until the top turns a light golden brown. Like all Southern dishes, this one should be served piping hot while the crust is still flaky."

The first summer I went to Edisto, Julia cooked for me. Nearly all the Island Negroes excel in cooking seafood, but Julia's diamond-back terrapin soup was so delicious and unusual I tried to learn her recipe. With paper and pencil in my hand I followed her about: "Now, Julia, tell me exactly how you make your terrapin soup."

"Yuh cooks yuh terr'pin with duh bay leaf e thyme, den yuh picks out all duh bones. Den yuh adds duh t'ck cream et nutmeg et jist fore yuh et add de Sherry wine."

"How much cream do I use, Julia?"

"Jist a 'ittle."

"But how much is a little?"

"Shucks, chile, ef e don' know how much is a 'ittle, yuh jist ain't no cook."

Julia prepared another famous Edisto dish called "Kedgeree." It is made from extra large bass or other fish that have grown so large the meat is coarse and is not good broiled, fried, or baked. Kedgeree, too, is delicious.

> 1 cup cooked rice
> 4 cups flaked raw fish
> 3 hard boiled eggs
> ½ cup melted butter
> 1 teaspoon salt

Dash of red pepper and enough cream to moisten. Bake 45 minutes in slow oven.

Not long ago, I saw Julia in a store on the Island and asked, "Julia, now can you tell me how much a little is?"

She laughed and held out her hand slightly cupped. "Missus, I still measure in this way, whether it's for one or twenty."

Rice cooked the Edisto way is dry and flaky, with every grain separate. The Negroes use no special pan to prepare it; such a thing as a rice steamer is unknown to them. They just put some water on the rice and cook it. If you ask how much water to use, the answer is the invariable "Jist a 'ittle." You try it that way, and you get a sticky mass no one will eat. I've often wondered if a bit of conjure is used.

III

From the tidal creeks, inlets, and rivers come crab, shrimp, and fish — the bases for dishes that are the Negroes' specialties. They are a skillful blend of traditional Edisto Island plantation recipes mixed by gifted hands into unforgettable dishes. The following are copied exactly as they appeared in the old cook books.

Tamer's Crab Soup

2 cups crab meat
2 hard-boiled eggs
2 cups rich milk
1 cup cream
2 tablespoon butter
1 teaspoon flour
Season with salt and pepper to taste
1 tablespoon sherry

Cook crabs until tender, about 20 minutes, in boiling salted water. Clean and pick meat and put in pan set in hot water. Add butter and 1½ cups milk. Simmer five minutes. Make paste of flour and remaining cup of milk. Stir slowly into first mixture. Cook over low heat 20 minutes. Add cream, chopped eggs, and sherry and serve.

Brown Oyster Stew

¼ lb. fat cooking bacon
(Butts meat)
2 tablespoon flour
2 onions, finely chopped
1 pt. oysters

Cut fat in small cubes. Fry out grease. Add flour, and brown. Add onions (brown, do not burn). Add 2 cups water.

Stir until smooth and slightly thick. Add oysters. When oysters are hot and curl, season to taste with salt and pepper. Serve immediately. (Long cooking toughens oysters.)

EDISTO OYSTER STEW

1 quart fresh oysters
1 cup liquid from oysters
1½ tablespoon butter
1 tablespoon flour
2 cups milk
4 tablespoon cream
Dash of mace
Salt and pepper

Scald oysters in liquid. Mix well butter, flour, and milk, and let come to boil. Add to oysters, then add cream. Season and serve hot.

CHICKEN-CRAB GUMBO

1 large hen
1 cup crab meat
1 cup sliced okra
1 large onion cut fine
Salt
Pepper
1 cup diced ham
3 tablespoons bacon fat

Remove from chicken both dark and light meat. Make a broth of skin and bones, cooking several hours, then cool. Cut up raw chicken meat into large pieces. Brown onion in bacon fat. Add chicken meat, diced ham, crab meat (shrimp can be used instead of crab and okra). Simmer mixture 15 minutes. Add chicken broth (about 4½ cups), cover, and let cook slowly two hours. Season to taste with salt and pepper. Serve with rice.

RED RICE

½ lb. sliced fat bacon
1½ cups rice
12 large tomatoes (canned ones will do)
1 red pepper ⎫
2 green peppers ⎬ All chopped fine
1 large onion ⎭

Fry out bacon in iron skillet. Toast rice in grease, stirring occasionally until it is a golden brown; add tomatoes, peppers, onion, salt and pepper to taste. Let simmer until rice is tender and flaky.

BLEAK HALL SALAD

Boil a turkey in salted water until tender. Let stand in broth until cold.

4 cups white meat of turkey (diced)
1½ cups palmetto heart sliced thin
8 hard boiled eggs (chopped)

Mix with dressing and serve cold.

DRESSING

3 tablespoons vinegar
¼ teaspoon salt
2 tablespoon flour
1 teaspoon mustard
2 teaspoon sugar
1 well-beaten egg

Mix all ingredients and cook until quite thick in pan set in water. Add one cup of stiffly whipped cream, measured before whipping.

PALMETTO HEART PICKLE

3 palmetto hearts
1½ lbs. onions.
1½ lbs. cabbage

Have three large palmetto trees cut and cabbage removed. Peel outside leaves from around hearts, using only the center. Slice in thin slices. Chop onions and cabbage in small pieces. Let stand in salt water 12 hours. Squeeze all water out. Put in pot and cover with mild vinegar. Add 1 tablespoon celery seed, 2 tablespoon mustard seed, 3 tablespoon dry mustard, 1 tablespoon turmeric, 2 cups sugar, 4 tablespoon flour. Add all ingredients except turmeric and flour. Cream turmeric and flour with little warm vinegar. Simmer all together 10 minutes, seal.

GREEN ORANGE MARMALADE

1 lb. oranges

1¾ lb. best crushed sugar

Grate oranges and then throw them in strong salt water, leaving them in for a night. Rinse thoroughly; then cut and squeeze the juice. Put seeds in one vessel and cover them with cold water to form a jelly, and put the juice in another. Take pulp out with a spoon, and add to the juice. Then boil skins in as many waters as will extract the bitter and make them so soft they can be mashed with a fork in a marble mortar. Add sugar to this mashed part, and leave until next morning. If oranges are very juicy put ⅔ juice, all pulp and jelly squeezed from seed. Boil until very thick. A blade of mace improves it. Be sure to put a little pinch of soda in the first two boilings. The water must be changed quickly and always put on hot or the skins will toughen.

MRS. BAILEY'S SOUR ORANGE PRESERVES

Grate orange peel slightly, all over orange. Put whole orange in salt brine for 12 to 16 hours, then take out and wash thoroughly in plain water, let boil 5 minutes, change water, and boil again 5 minutes. If still bitter, change water again and boil five minutes. To 1 lb. oranges add 1½ lbs. sugar. Let boil slowly until oranges become transparent.

Maum Rachel

SHORTLY after the end of the Confederate War, a young doctor fresh out of medical school settled on Edisto Island. The white people welcomed him, and he spent many pleasant hours as a guest in their homes, but they were of sturdy stock and seldom had need of his professional services. The hundreds of Negroes on the Island spoke politely to him in passing, but not one knocked on the little schoolhouse door where he had established his office and living quarters. Since a time beyond memory, Maum Rachel had helped birth and doctor the black people with skill — and often a little conjure. They saw no reason to change.

Even up at the big house Maum Rachel was always present when her beloved Mistress' babies were born, and her hands were the first to bathe and dress them. Her keen eyes watched every move the doctor made, and what she saw she added to her own practice.

As her daughter Mandy's time drew near old Maum Rachel was worried. Mandy was doing poorly, despite the birthing charm Maum Rachel had sewed in a clean white cloth for Mandy to wear around her neck.

Maum Rachel wondered if somebody was trying to conjure Mandy. It wasn't the time of year for a rattlesnake to shed; but one morning when the old woman started out the door the ghostly long gray length of a snakeskin was stretched across the steps in the morning sun. She just missed putting her foot on it. Hurriedly she retreated into the house and put a pot of water on the fire. Then, carrying a shovel, she went out the back door, and all the way around the house to the front where the snakeskin lay. It was so old and brittle it broke into hundreds of pieces, and some blew away like thistledown as she slid the shovel underneath the skin. "Dat's trouble," she muttered to herself.

Once more circling the house, she entered the back door with the shovel stretched before her. After dumping the pieces of dried snakeskin into the pot, she unlocked a drawer in her old bureau and removed several small dark objects — a dried toad, the roots of some herbs, and a bottle of liquid. These joined the snakeskin, while the old woman stirred the pot and mumbled a few strange words. Maum Rachel watched intently for a moment, then a satisfied smile broke on her face, and she carried the concoction outside. Dipping a brush broom in the pot, she scrubbed the step where she had found the snake.

For weeks Maum Rachel had been watching the spider spin its web in the smoke-blackened rafters near the fire. This was a lucky omen, for often one had to go to a dozen houses before finding a home spider's web. She had taken extra care that not a flake of soot on the web was disturbed, for as every good midwife knew, it was necessary that it be held together with plenty of soot. Sometimes the mother's life depended on having a good spider's web handy.

Mandy's son, ten-year-old James, was in the yard sharpening the ploughshare. First he scrubbed it with coarse sand; then he sharpened it until it would split a hair from the old ox's tail at the slightest touch. When the birthing was near, it would be placed under the bed where its sharp edge would cut the pains. Some claimed an axe was better, but Rachel had learned from her grandmother that the ploughshare was safer.

Maum Rachel had plenty of dried herbs on hand, and for several days she had been busy scrubbing and washing. Sweet, clean sheets were stacked in a pile on top of an old chest, and the copper kettle was polished bright as a new penny. Outside, the wood which James had spent days in cutting was piled high, and there was plenty of lightwood ready to burst into flame at the touch of a match. Now all there was to do was to wait for the moon to full.

(115)

Mandy's day dawned bright and clear, without a streak of red in the sky. Maum Rachel was glad. If a baby first opens its eyes on a stormy day and hears the northeast wind groaning and sweeping across the marsh, it is bound for trouble. But the day wore on, the tide rose and fell, the moon came up, and Mandy grew weaker and weaker despite all her mother's help. Even the strong ergot tea which had never failed Maum Rachel before seemed to have lost its power, and she wondered if she dared give Mandy another dose. With trembling hands she shook the bottle hard and pouring a spoonful carried it to the bed. A grayish look on the black face of the girl struck terror to the mother's heart. "E open e mouth, jist a little," pleaded the old woman. Mandy's jaw dropped loosely, the liquid ran out the corner of her mouth and made a dark reddish-brown stain, like old blood, on the white homespun pillowcase.

With tears in her eyes Maum Rachel turned from the bed. Pushing her way through the silent women in the next room, she reached the door and beckoned to a youngster standing with the men in the moonlit yard. "Jeems, e go fur de nu doct. Trabbel fast fer when de maunin come et de tide turn e be to late."

It was midnight when the doctor reached the cabin. The black people around the front door separated and left a pathway for him. The girl was barely breathing, and as the doctor leaned over her, Maum Rachel said despondently, "Deh only one chance lef, Massa. Yunnah better mek 'ace and quill er; de tide near full."

"Quill her?" said the young doctor slowly, hesitating to show his ignorance. He knew only that the girl was dying, and he was powerless to help her. But during his short stay on the Island he had come to know the Island Negroes and to respect their ways. What the old woman wanted to do would bring comfort to her and could not harm the girl. "You do it, Maum Rachel," he said, "and I'll help if you need me."

Half-blinded by tears that streamed down her withered cheeks, Maum Rachel stumbled to the mantel and took a long goose quill from a fruit jar. Two of the women raised Mandy's head, while the old woman took from a pocket in her apron a small tin box and removed a pinch of snuff. With the snuff held in front of the quill she leaned over the girl and blew strongly, directly in the patient's face. Mandy gave a mighty sneeze — and the birthing was over.

The exhausted girl sank back upon the pillow, and her eyes closed. Now the doctor knew what to do. He hastily injected stimulants, and Mandy's eyes slowly opened, but they were glazed and expressionless. Before the doctor could interfere, Maum Rachel placed a cupped hand on each side of the girl's mouth and blew her own breath into her child's body. Together, Maum Rachel and the young doctor had saved the girl's life.

Years afterward, when the doctor had gone from Edisto he told a classmate the story of another night on the Island. A very old Negro had been taken desperately ill, and as the young physician sat by the patient with no sound except the heavy breathing of the sick man, a gust of wind had come through the open window and blown out the candle, leaving only the faintest moonlight in the room. Suddenly there was a sound of rustling, fluttering wings, and "there appeared in the window, poised in the air, a spectre fanning its wings which outstretched were wider than the window frame. It carried two great balls of fire above the wings." The doctor felt a chill run up his spine; he gave an involuntary yell, and "the apparition passed away in the darkness."

When the occupants of the next room opened the door and brought a light they found the old man dead. Had an owl been attracted by the light and fanned it out as it flew in the window?

But no one saw an owl, and the older Negroes say that a huge black bird appears at a man's death to carry his spirit on.

Sara

HIGH BALL PIKE goes from the beach to Dawhoo Bridge. It runs through Seaside and the Burrough; then, crossing Russel Creek, it stretches through the salt marshes on Little Edisto. The Negroes gave the road its present name when it was paved and automobiles started to "high-ball" down to the beach.

Palmetto Road cuts off the Pike near the beach, winding several miles through the woods down to "The Neck," where the Whaleys and Edingses once lived. Along the road and back among the trees there are numbers of Negro cabins. Far off in the dense woods, where huge rattlesnakes grow as many as twelve rattles and it is almost impossible for a white man to find his way, it is said that the Negroes make a powerful drink called "scrap iron."

Sara Reese was born eighty-five years ago in a house near Palmetto Road. When she was seventeen she married young Gaddy, and he was considered the luckiest boy in Seaside, for Sara's savory conch stew was the envy of all the women on the road, and no other house matched hers in cleanliness or held so many fine patchwork quilts. Sara was thrifty, too, and she and her husband worked in the field side by side. They had several children, but Sara's first-born, Rufe, was her pride. When Gaddy died, Rufe took his place as head of the family, and like his father he proved to be a good provider. He had been taught to run a straight furrow and keep his cotton free from weeds; and when winter came, strings of onions hung from the rafters and jars of home-raised vegetables lined the kitchen shelves.

Under the eaves of the house where it would catch the rainwater, Rufe put a barrel half-filled with oak ashes. When the water had drawn the lye from the ashes, the liquid was strained and poured over whole grains of corn. Twenty-four hours later, the husks were easily removed, and Rufe and

Sara had the much relished lye hominy. Sara would fry out butt's meat, and add the hominy to the smoking fat to cook. Hominy and butt's meat, eaten with any seafood, made Rufe's favorite dish.

Rufe cultivated a small patch of rice each year, and enough peas and seva beans to last from planting to planting. In the corner of the garden, sweet potatoes were banked with cornstalks cleverly arranged on tops to shed water. Rufe kept the outside of the small house shining clean with whitewash and helped his mother tend the beds of flowers that grew in the yard. There was contentment, industry, and happiness.

It pleased Rufe's mother when he married his cousin Kathy. The women worked well together, and the little house was filled with song and laughter. Kathy saved soap wrappers and sent them off to the city, and the day the big box containing the premiums arrived was a happy time. Sara and Kathy eagerly unwrapped each piece of glassware, holding it up to the light, and exclaiming together over its beauty. Sara, as she watched the girl wash the glasses in a huge basin of soapy water and polish each one until it shined, was content. More and more she let Kathy take over the running of the little household. At times, at Kathy's urging, she even took her ease on the front gallery, dreaming in the sun and watching the play of light in the gray moss hanging from the trees, as her daughter-in-law busied herself inside.

But Kathy died when her second child was born. Sara grieved for her like she was her own.

The years passed swiftly. Sara took up her old duties and brought up Rufe's two children. Then, they married, and Rufe and Sara were alone again. It troubled Rufe to see his mother work so hard. Perhaps it was dreams of the old happy times with Kathy that made him marry Ellie and bring her home.

From the beginning, Ellie hated Sara and Sara was irritated by Ellie's slovenly ways. Sara saw her soft clean quilts become torn and dirty. The floor no longer had the whiteness of beach sand, and the poorly cooked food sickened her. Sometimes a sigh would escape her — an involuntary "Ooh — Ooh."

Ellie was quick to resent it. "Don't 'Ooh' at me ole woman," she would scream. "I ain't no owl. My feet ain't fit no limb."

Rufe lost all interest in farming, and the garden grew high in weeds. At last he went to work for wages on the highway. Ellie did not let her husband hear her speak unkindly to his mother, but with Rufe gone all day she unleashed her hatred. When the old woman became bedridden Ellie taunted her with her helplessness. At times she would break a piece of Sara's prized glassware before her eyes — just to see the misery in them. At times she would burst into fits of rage and even strike the defenseless woman. Sara seldom spoke, but everywhere Ellie went she felt the old eyes following her.

The tide was low about six o'clock one hot August morning. Sammy Gaddy, on his way to get crabs out of the creek back of Palmetto Road, joined his Uncle Rufe and walked with him on his way to work along the narrow dirt road that leads to the highway. They stood talking a few minutes when they reached the Pike, and after they parted Sammy went down to the creek. Carrying a stout stick, he waded in the pluff mud and sniffed the welcome odor. The mud oozed between his toes and made him feel cool, clear up to his head. If a bubble rose in the mud he knew there was a crab under it; then, if the stick was pushed down gently, the crab would grab it and he could easily catch it.

When a weird moan drifted through the woods, Sammy thought it was a dove. But it came again and again. "Dat's uh strange ting dat sound e trabbel wid me," Sammy said aloud. "Dat sparit sure ken mak sight ob noise dis hear maunin."

He busied himself with his work and the sound ceased. "I'se sure glad e got rid ob 'um," Sammy said.

The sun rose higher and blazed down in golden splendor. Sammy leisurely filled the old bean basket with crabs. When it was full he lifted it to his shoulder and started home. Near Rufe's house he saw a crowd of people in the doorway and the yard. Shrieks and cries came from the house, and he went inside. Sara was on the bed, swarms of flies on her face and on the coagulating pool of blood beside her. But none of it bothered Sara, for she was dead. An axe covered with her blood was on the floor.

Ellie fled to the swamps. Days later she was arrested on the streets of Charleston.

"Sparits"

SOME of the medley of African voodoo brought to the Island by the slaves over a hundred and fifty years ago undoubtedly is still practiced by the Negroes in a small way. Many of the customs and beliefs have gone with the passing of the older generations, but all the Negroes are superstitious, especially concerning the dead. And superstition is not confined to the colored race alone. A highly intelligent and cultured white gentleman, whose forebears were among the early settlers says he often sees the "little people," as he calls them, on his plantation. They wave to him in friendly fashion, but if an outsider intrudes they fade away in the eerie gray shadows of the moss-hung trees.

The Negroes paint their doors and shutters a bright blue to keep out evil spirits. (It is said that in the early days they used the skimming from the indigo pots.) "Sparits," the

Negroes claim, are able to assume all kinds of shapes; after midnight the dead rise from their graves and walk in the form of goats, dogs, and other animals. It is almost impossible to get some of the Edisto Negroes to pass certain places after dark. Certain old women have the power to make "love charms" and to cast spells that cause sickness and sometimes death. Dried frogs, snakes, lizards, and black cats are used to brew concoctions suitable for various purposes.

I went to Mary's house one morning to bring her to work, and as she sat down in the back of the car a bumble bee stung her on her wrist and it began to swell. I have never seen anyone so upset. "Enty, e put um dere fur me," Mary gasped; and that's all I could get her to say.

All day she worried, but the next morning the swelling had disappeared, and I heard no more about it. I have no doubt she went to see an old "conjur woman" and paid her for a charm to break the spell.

Another day, I asked her if she had ever seen a ghost. "Mebbe yunnah ain't believe me, Missus," she replied, "but Vic [her sister] she see plent ob dem sparits."

"How do they look, Mary?"

"Vic, she say duh feet turn back'ards and dey nebber tech groun' an' dey blow dey hot breat' down yuh neck."

It is seldom the Negroes will admit a personal experience. "Ghost ain't like fur yuh to talk 'um," they say. But if you can persuade them to talk, they will tell you of others — their relatives and friends — who have had fearful experiences with "sparits." Bill Doctor, who has lived on Pine Baron plantation many years, will occasionally tell of ghosts. One summer night several years ago, Mrs. W——, awakening suddenly, found the heat was so intense that she went out on the wide screened veranda to cool off. The late moon was shining brightly, spotting the yard with alternate patches of light and shadow. Suddenly, to her surprise, Mrs. W—— saw a man on horseback cross the yard about two hundred feet from the house, then disappear into the darkness.

When Bill came to work several hours later, she said, "Bill, you did not get much sleep last night; you were out until nearly morning."

"No'm," answered the old man, "I go straight home from here. Rosie [his wife] she not feeling so well. I stay with she."

"Some one crossed the yard just before daylight. I thought it was you."

"No'm. Dat was the dead in hurry to get back to de Mikell graveyard fore day-clean. Dey stay way too long en tak short cut through yuh yard."

Carrie Smith told me of an evening when she and her husband sat with several friends on her doorsteps at first dusk. A short distance away stood an old store building, where an accident had occurred a few weeks before. Susan Sanders, who kept the store, had been accidentally shot by Lil' Pa Gadston. While Carrie and her friends talked together in the dusk, they saw a figure move swiftly across the Smith yard a few paces away. Its feet were off the ground, and it seemed to float.

"Who dat?" asked one.

"I ain't know who," said another.

"Dat's Susan," Carrie said, as the figure faded through the closed store door. "E done fergit somethin' and come for it."

Carrie told me that spirits had chased her and thrown water in her face; sometimes they rolled up in a ball and bounced along the road, kicking up clouds of dust.

I tried to get Molly Brown who lives up in the Burrough to talk about spirits. She is very old, and I have been told she makes charms and casts spells. "Molly," I asked, "when you were young, did anyone every try to conjure you?"

A cautious closed look came over her face. "E don't believe in sich, Missus," she said.

I stayed a little longer talking about various things and finally repeated the story of an experience with spirits one of her friends had told me.

"E duh 'member, Missus, de time e see sparit if yuh want ter hear 'bout ghos'. We'en, my broth'r and I, been young muh mummy went to church on duh Sabbath. She tole us tuh stay 'ome. We'en wait wile, den tak path thru woods.

"Well, Missus, I scacely gone enyway fore uh big gray man stood in de mid'l ob de path. E wore tall beav'r hat et e spread e arms wide et we'en couldn't pass. Just back of he wuz de big'est rattlesnake I eber see. We'en sho run dat day, and de ghos' sho save we'en from snake dat time!"

II

When I went to Edisto many years ago, I engaged Toria to be my laundress. When she showed signs of illness that simple remedies would not cure, I offered to take her to a doctor in Charleston, but she refused to go.

"T'ain't no use, Missus," she said sadly, "I gwine see death. Beula, e done hab ole Riah f'row spell puntop me. Jist yestiddy top do'step uh fin' dried toad. T'ain't no use."

I had heard of Mariah and of her reputation for making conjure charms. I decided to go see her — first, to use diplomacy and, if unsuccessful, to try to frighten the old woman so she would stop harrassing Toria.

After a ride of two miles over a narrow sandy road I found Riah's cabin standing in a small clearing. I stood in the doorway and waited for my eyes to become accustomed to the semi-darkness. The shutters were tightly closed, and the faint light from the open door and from the fire gave the room the shadows of twilight. Then I saw Riah sitting in a low chair in front of a large fireplace. There was an iron pot hanging over the fire, and a musty odor filled the room.

A long-stemmed pipe hung between the woman's toothless gums. She stared at me silently, and her beady black eyes never left my face, nor did her blank expression change.

I had an almost irresistible desire to turn and run. Finally, mustering my courage, I said, "Riah, I want to talk with you about Toria and ask you to stop bothering her."

Her answer surprised me. "Daughtuh," she said, "Yuh ain't 'fraid old Riah?"

"No," I answered untruthfully, and I handed her two bags of tobacco and several small pieces of silver. Her lips spread in a grin, and her claw-like fingers grabbed the bribe; "Fuh sutt'n, Missus, Riah help Toria. Tell she attuh w'ile she be well. Riah suh so."

I delivered the message to Toria, and indeed Toria did begin to mend. In a short time she was completely well.

Beulah had fallen in love with Toria's husband Bi'man. She used every know means to lure him away from Toria, but Bi'man resisted all of Beulah's wiles. Whenever Beulah passed Bi'man in the road, she claimed, "E suck e tee't at me," an indication of scorn unbearable to the Island Negro. Beulah decided to get revenge.

When Bi'man complained of steadily increasing pains in his chest, Toria tearfully begged me to go see Riah again. They had heard of Beulah's threats to get even, and felt sure she had paid Riah to work a conjure. I could not refuse to go, but I felt rather foolish as I reluctantly started on the trip. When I entered Riah's cabin she looked as if she had not moved since I left her weeks before. This time, she received me politely: "Maunin', Missus, how yuh do, Ma'am?"

In addition to tobacco, I had carried her some groceries. The moment she saw them she arose and went to an old chest in the corner of the room. Pulling out a drawer she drew forth a corncob doll, crudely made to resemble a man. The arms and legs were match stems and the head a small piece of wood fastened to the body with a rusty wire. A flannel string, smelling strongly of kerosene, was wrapped tightly around the doll's chest. She unwound the string and told me

(125)

to take the doll to Toria, and to tell her to keep it and no "sparits" would ever harm her family.

Although I had not mentioned the reason for my visit, Riah had known it instantly. I cannot believe that an old black woman slowly unwinding a kerosene-soaked string from around a corncob doll could cure a sick man; but Bi'man's pains immediately ceased.

III

Nearly fifteen years ago Joe Simmons came to Edisto from Coosau Island, near Beaufort. The young Negro had saved several hundred dollars, and with it he bought twenty-five acres of fine farming land. He salvaged an old shrimp boat, and during the season he would bring in his boat loaded with bushels of fine prawns, even when other fishermen caught little.

When Joe married Melia, they spent their wedding night in a new home. Joe had fashioned it with his own hands. There were three rooms, and a lean-to covering the pump, so that Melia would not have to carry water up the steps — a luxury no other colored woman on the Island enjoyed. Bright-hued linoleum covered the floors in the rooms, and all the furniture had come from Charleston and was brand new.

Joe and Melia's little son was three years old when Tamey and her old mother, with Tamey's three children, moved down to Seaside, across the road from Joe and Melia. They were blue-gum Negroes from up in the Burrough, and their neighbors had sighed with relief at seeing them go, for they were quarrelsome and mean.

From the beginning the newcomers envied the happy little family across the way and deliberately the two women laid their plans. Tamey always had an errand to Joe's house when he was home. When Melia again became heavy with child, the old woman spent long hours stirring brews to put in delicacies, which Tamey took to Melia. While Melia ate,

Tamey filled her ear with stories of death and the dangers of childbirth. Melia would break out in a cold sweat. She could not understand why she felt so sad and unhappy — so different from the time she carried little Joe.

From a cousin of Melia I got the end of the story. When the baby was due the old woman offered her services, and Melia was never well afterwards.

One morning Joe came for Melia's cousin before day. The baby had died. He did not know what to do. Would she come and see if she could help Melia?

Long before they reached the house they heard Melia singing a plaintive "make-up" song:

> Oh Lord have mercy on me
> Lord have mercy on me
> Lord have mercy on me
> Oh — Oh Lord have mercy on me.
>
> Oh yes e take my baby an e gone
> Oh yes e take my baby an e gone
> Lord have mercy on me
> Oh — Oh Lord have mercy on me.

On and on the sad tearful voice sang — on through the day and the night, the next day and the night. Finally, there was nothing else for Joe to do but to take the poor woman to the state hospital, where she died.

But Tamey never lived in the comfortable little house she had coveted. Joe carried his little son to his mother on Coosau, and Edisto saw him no more.

IV

It was Palm Sunday. A mocking bird sat in the Cassina bush near the church and preened himself. He puffed his feathers and cocked his head, bright inquisitive eyes looking one way and then another. In a few minutes he began to sing. The melody came through the open windows into the

(127)

church and mingled with the voices of the choir. The air was heavy with the odor of the yellow jessamine that hung in masses from the magnolia trees, and its rich fragrance pervaded the old church. The organ music ceased, and the mocking bird, too, was silent, as the aged rector raised his arms: "The peace of God, which passeth all understanding, keep your hearts and minds in the knowledge and love of God, and of his Son Jesus Christ, our Lord; and the blessings of God Almighty, the Father, the Son, and the Holy Ghost, be amongst you and remain with you always. Amen."

The service was over. As the congregation moved slowly into the churchyard the midday sun blazed down on them, its shining rays touching the graves like a benediction. On one side of the church stood carriages and high-spirited horses, impatiently pawing the earth, thinking of the green pastures waiting for them at home; but the planters and their families were in no hurry. Eager to learn the news of the past week, they gathered in groups with relatives and friends. A frail, lovely lady walked alone toward her carriage. In her slender hand she held a tiny palm-cross, symbol of the crucifixion. An aged Negro, his white head uncovered, watched her approach. After assisting her to enter, he closed the carriage door, climbed up on the high seat, and gathered up the reins. The carriage rolled over a sandy road for several miles, then turned off on a lane that ran through broad cotton fields until it reached a wide tree-lined avenue that led to the big house.

The mistress of the house walked slowly up the steps. Just a year ago this day, its master had been laid to rest under great trees in sight of his home. Mrs. S—— paused a moment when she reached the porch. Resting her hand against one of the white columns, she looked toward the family burying ground. When she entered the hallway a tall gaunt Negro came forward. With the freedom of a privileged servant, he waited for her to speak, but the shaking old hands clutching his hat betrayed his agitation.

"Is anything wrong, Joe?" she asked kindly.

"Yes'm, Missus, Cissie she en bad way. Ole Sue done put 'bad mout' [spell or conjure] on she. Oh, Missus, cannuh yuh do somethin? Cissie won't eat a mout'ful. I try every t'ing I knows. E jist can't stan um if Cissie, she die. She all I got since 'er ma gone. Please, Missus, help ole Joe." Tears ran down his cheeks, and his pleading eyes looked into hers.

"Wait a minute Joe, and I will go with you." Mrs. S—— opened her bag and withdrew a small object from it. With Joe a few steps behind her, she walked down "de street" that ran through the Negro quarters. The doorways filled with dusky peering faces as she passed, and murmuring voices queried one another. It was unusual for Mistress to walk out in the noonday sun.

In Joe's cabin, his daughter lay motionless, and her eyes were closed. The spotlessly clean bed had been drawn beneath the window overlooking the marsh. Out there, among the swaying green grass the harsh cry of a heron broke the stillness as the great white bird flapped its way like a departing spirit toward the sea. Inside the hot cabin, a frayed yellow palm-leaf fan lay on a table by the bed. Cissie's father had dropped it there when he went for his mistress. Throughout the night and morning he had sat by the bed, keeping the air gently stirring around the girl's fevered brow.

All her life, Mrs. S—— had lived on a large plantation surrounded by hundreds of Negroes. She was familiar with their superstitions and vivid imaginations. She knew they could brood over imagined curses and spells until they actually felt the symptoms they had been threatened with. Looking at Cissie, she knew that the girl did not need a doctor or medicine, but that fear must be removed from her mind if she were to live.

"Cissie!" Mrs. S—— spoke sharply. The girl opened her eyes but did not answer. Then, very slowly and gently Mrs. S—— placed the tiny palm-cross she had brought from the church in Cissie's hand. "Here is something that is more powerful than any evil thing," she said kindly and firmly. "Wear it over your heart until night comes, and when the moon is full burn it carefully so that not an ash is left. Eat the broth I send you, and in the morning you will be well."

A few days later Cissie was at work in the field.

The Ebb and the Flow

IN HIS book *Rumbling of the Chariot Wheels* the late Jenkins Mikell tells of a tragedy that occurred among the Negroes on his father's Edisto plantation, Peter's Point, or Point St. Pierre.

"Early one morning, we were awakened by the repressed excitement we felt around the dwelling. We soon found that all our people on the home place were in a terribly wrought-up state and waiting for the Master to appear. A murder had been committed among them. A man had killed his wife in anger. The poor woman had been found dead hanging by her neck to the rafter of their cabin, and the guilty husband had run away and left her there. He was caught during the day. As the nearest jail was forty miles away, in Charleston, and, as the next steamer to the city would not go for a week, the duty of guarding the prisoner devolved on the Master. He had a large cage built, in which the murderer was kept until he could be removed to the jail. In time he was tried and convicted and remanded to the scene of his crime for execution. Again the awful duty of being his jailer was ours. On the day of execution very little work was done in the community by the Negroes. All attended the tragic scene. His coffin was made on the plantation and placed in a wagon. The doomed man, tied, seated upon this coffin, rode six miles to the place of execution, and by his side, seated on the same gruesome seat was his companion in guilt — a woman. She was made to witness, at close quarters, his dreadful end. She returned to the place of burial on the plantation seated on the box containing his dead body, and as it was lowered into the grave, she was seized by a frenzied mob, forced into the open pit, and every effort was made to bury her alive. These efforts nearly succeeded. But wiser counsels prevailed and she was at last released. The moral responsibility resting on the head of a large slave owner was, at times, a terrible one. To a conscientious man it was always sobering."

Several small Piccalos, as the Negroes call them, dot the Island. Here on Friday and Saturday nights the colored people gather in large numbers to dance, play cards, eat, and drink beer. These revelries usually last until early morning. Occasionally the merrymakers go, instead, to a home where the owner sells fried fish sandwiches and drinks, but since these affairs are attended only by invitation, the Piccalos are more popular.

Sometimes tragedy enters the dance halls. One Saturday night, Phinnie, a young woman from the Burrough, came down to Viola's Piccalo in Seaside. The place was crowded. At times the dancers seemed scarcely to move their feet; only their bodies swayed in time with the music. The air in the room was heavy with smoke and the smell of stale beer.

The strains of the music filtered out of the dance hall to the highway, as Phinnie's husband stepped inside. He stood motionless; when several friends spoke to him he stared ahead and did not seem to hear. Phinnie danced on, moving with young abandoned grace and having no thought except "pleasuring herself." She was unaware that her husband was near until he grabbed her arm and pulled her out into the darkness. Phinnie's husband stabbed her three times, and she died. The Piccalo played on, but no one danced again that night.

The Negroes know every inlet and creek around the island and can designate them by name. They know where the big bass feed, and where to find trout, sheepshead, and drum. They know where clam beds lie, and where the plump white-foot oysters thrive. In the spring I have seen Lucas Munjin come in with his boat loaded with Norfolk spots, when we thought we had good fishing with a string of twenty.

Some years ago, "the government, carrying out a Board of Fisheries project through their agents, hired local Negroes to reseed the old oyster beds that were fast becoming extinct. The agents were amazed to find the Negroes could tell at a glance the number of bushels of oysters piled high in a boat." Careful checking seldom disclosed an error in their estimates.

Before automobiles bumped over every narrow, sand-rutted road, the Negroes on the Island had their own special telegraph system. Up in the Burrough or down in Seaside, if a death occurred, day or night, a wail would come from the house of sorrow: "Mossy, she muddah e gone! Tell Mossy she muddah e gone!" At the next house the words would be taken up, and on and on the message would go, carried by human voices riding the wind. Out in the fields, on the road, or on bypaths, men and women would hearken; then cry the lugubrious news until it reached its destination on the other side of the Island, informing the bereaved ones of their loss.

Today, the lives of the black people on the Island are still governed by the moon, wind, and tide. Life goes out with the ebb, and new life comes in with the young flood. No self-respecting fish will bite when the wind sweeps in from the east, and certain crops must be planted by stages of the moon. In some ways, things have not changed.

Island Ways

Christmas on Edisto

CHRISTMAS on Edisto — how truly charming it must have been! The houses were filled with family and guests. The odor of spicy mince pies, hickory-smoked hams and corn-fattened turkeys, all baking in a huge oven, filled the air. Bowls of eggnog were heaped high with thick cream and sprinkled liberally with nutmeg. The pantry shelves were lined with pies and cakes; and out in the smokehouses, along with dozens of hams, were hung legs of venison and beef, and long chains of link sausage ready to accompany the batter cakes at breakfast.

In the midst of all the holiday preparations, the loud clear whistle of the steamboat stopped every activity, and a rush was made to reach the landing in time to greet the son or daughter returning from college in the North to spend Christmas at home. Then the Island really became merry, as the young people went from house to house greeting cousins and older relatives. There were charades and dances, moonlight rides and picnics — perhaps a promise given, to be fulfilled, when summer came, in old St. Stephens church on Edingsville.

During the golden era before 1860 the holiday festivities on Edisto lasted from a week before Christmas through New Year's day. The time was spent in hunts, banquets, dances, and horse racing. Every plantation stable held several fine blooded horses, and there was great rivalry between owners. The slaves shared in the gaiety; all field work ceased on the plantations, and extra allowances of fruits and sweets were issued. Songs were sung in the churches and in the numerous Negro praise houses. It was a time of happiness for all.

In the large entrance hall of each planter's home a tall green cedar tipped the high ceiling. The tree was decorated with garlands of popcorn and ropes of looped colored paper, and tapers made on the plantation of the wax of Marsh

Myrtle berries made flickering lights. Wreaths of Cassina, often called Christmas berry, heavy with bright red fruit hung from the front door, and mistletoe was placed over the wide doorways inside.

At seven o'clock on Christmas morning the farm bell was rung — a signal for master, mistress, and house servants to join the children around the tree. The candles cast a soft light over the eager faces as the master said a short prayer. Then the merriment started with the giving out of the gifts; no one was forgotten, and many were the greetings and thanks that echoed throughout the house.

The late Jenkins Mikell has left a record of a Christmas gathering long ago at Bleak Hall. The invitation to the affair was issued at church on the Sunday before Christmas by Colonel Townsend's saying, "We hope to see you and yours on the 27th to join us in our Christmas festivities — an oyster roast." Mr. Mikell relates that the roast was no more than the salad course, so to speak, in the entertainment.

"On the day before the 27th all arrangements were made: rustic tables and seats were put in place; cords of oak, hickory, and cedar made ready for the torch. The roads and the long causeways leading to Botany Bay were smoothed off and put in order for the carriages of the guests. Botany Bay was an adjunct to the plantation, an island of wild oaks, palmettoes and cedar, a tropical jungle impenetrable twenty yards from the beach, five miles long and a half-mile wide, inhabited by deer, marsh tackeys, wild hogs and half-wild cattle (hence the name 'Botany Bay').

"The beach was unsurpassed on the Atlantic coast. White-foot oysters obtained a few yards from the beach, were left in salt water until the last minute, to preserve their flavor and tang of the sea. They were named after the tribe of White-foot Indians, a subdivision of the Edistoes, who claimed and maintained their dominion over the territory in many a hard fought battle."

At one o'clock great barrels of oysters were poured on live coals. Mr. Mikell describes the feast: "As the guests seated themselves, they found an individual place mat of coarse linen to hold wooden platters of oysters, an oyster cloth on the left, an oyster knife with protective guard on the right. A tumbler for each was not left off. First came the butler, with a steaming pitcher filling the glasses with hot old time 'knock down — drag out' punch made of lemons, hot water, sugar and double-proof, imported Irish peat whiskey. The lighter wines were in reserve for the main course — the dinner proper. A dozen little pickaninnies rushed from the fire with platters filled with hot sputtering oysters and placed one before each person."

After the oysters were eaten, the guests strolled along the beach for an hour, and then returned to the table to find that a transformation had taken place. A heavy Irish linen cloth covered the table, and the place settings were of heavy silver. The dinner has been brought from the big house in carts. "Even to my childish mind its magnificance and prodigality were striking," Mr. Mikell writes. "At three o'clock in the afternoon we took our seats, at five we were still sitting — some unable to rise."

"*The Planters Occasionally Relax*"

THE old Edisto Islanders had many forms of entertainment. David Ramsay in his early history of South Carolina relates that dancing was a favorite amusement even before the Revolution and that "the planters occasionally relax themselves with games of coit, hand and trap-balls, but the recreation which engrosses more of their time and attention than any other is that of fishing."

Diaries tell of balls that began in the old military hall at eight in the evening and did not cease until sunrise, when the young people and their visitors would ride to one of the plantation houses for a breakfast of ham and eggs, hot biscuits, waffles and scones.

Each year tilts, or lancing tournaments, were held. Knight on horseback vied with knight in games of skill for the privilege of crowning his favorite lady "Queen of Love and Beauty." Each year the tournaments were held on a different plantation, where a bountiful midday feast was served. Afterwards, the men, dressed like knights of old with shining armour and waving plumes, rode their high-spirited horses, two abreast, to the scene of the tilt. There was the clanking of silver spurs, and the sunshine sparkled on the fine embroidered saddlecloths and silver-trimmed harnesses.

Weeks before the tournament, slaves were busy building a large covered platform for the judges and spectators. An old diary describes the tilt: "Three small rings, an inch and a quarter in diameter, were suspended from cross bars at regular intervals. The Knights galloped their horses and attempted to throw their lances through the rings. Each was allowed three chances and the course of 120 yards had to be covered in eight seconds or the rider was disqualified.

"When the tilt was over the riders again formed two abreast, and led by a trumpeter dressed in a red coat and three cornered hat, they passed by the reviewers' stands — this same trumpeter was the one who gave the order to 'charge' at the beginning of the tournament.

"It was an exciting moment when the winner was declared. He then proclaimed his choice for Queen and she was crowned. That night she reigned over the elaborate dance and was indeed 'belle of the ball.'"

Horse racing, too, was a favorite mode of entertainment. As early as 1788 the *State Gazette* reports that the Carolina Jockey Club "last Tuesday commenced the races at Parker's Ferry of Edisto." The Island racetracks were on the road that now turns off the highway to go to Bleak Hall. It is the only straightaway on the Island. Many of the young planters raced their fine blooded horses along this course, and many a gold piece changed hands afterwards.

The Edisto Yacht Club was one of the original members of the Sea Island Club. I could find no record of when it was founded, although an old newspaper clipping relates that in the early 1890's Jenkins Mikell of Edisto Island sailed his boat "Mermaid" and John Sosnowski his boat "Bohicket" over practically the same courses used today. As the races grew in popularity and others entered, people from Charleston and other Sea Islands anchored a short distance offshore to watch — later to join the festivities at Rockville, the starting point across the river from Edisto. Sometimes the races lasted for several days, and twenty-five or thirty boats would register for the series. Mishaps were frequent, ranging from torn sails and broken masts to capsizing. Sometimes choppy water and unfavorable winds caused many not to finish the contest. The regatta ended with the customary finale to almost all Island amusements — a dance, with coffee and sandwiches served at 2 A.M.

The Edisto Yacht Club has been inactive for years. The recently organized Edisto Beach Club last year purchased a graceful little boat and entered it in the local regatta. It finished the race with flying colors. It is hoped that continued success will revive the old-time enthusiasm, and that the colors will triumphantly wave in many a regatta.

Edingsville

EDINGSVILLE became a summer residence for the Edisto planters early in the nineteenth century. William Seabrook had just bought his plantation on the Island from William Brisbane, who in the space of a few years had made an enormous fortune planting Sea Island cotton. So great were Seabrook's profits on this staple, he cleared the purchase price in two years, besides adding to his holdings of slaves. The other planters prospered similarly, and long before 1820 there were sixty large, comfortable houses on Edingsville. Behind the houses were vegetable and flower gardens, carriage houses and slave quarters. Later, there were two churches and an academy. Edingsville was owned by the Edings family, and the land was leased to the other residents, usually for a period of ten years with the privilege of renewal, at an annual rent of four hundred dollars per lot.

The planters, without knowing the reason, had discovered that the cool sea breezes brought relief from the dreaded "country fever," so prevalent in the Low Country during the hot months. Early in May, great activity could be seen in the big houses on the plantations as preparations were made to move to the "Bay," as Edingsville was often called. Wagons and carts loaded with house servants and necessary equipment moved over the burning sandy roads, with the owners following in their carriages.

Long summer days were spent in swimming, sailing, dancing, giving teas, and entertaining friends from Charleston and the neighboring Sea Islands. For a few hours each weekday the planters rode home to assure themselves that all was well with their crops, but they returned in time for three o'clock dinner. It was a leisurely, carefree life — in deep contrast to those years that followed the War between the States.

But there was heartbreak as well as gaiety on Edingsville. Almost in sight of the ocean and near enough to hear the sound of the waves was a level stretch of ground known as "The Sands." Here many duels were fought, to satisfy pride or avenge a reflection on honor. Among the yellowed papers of a man who took part in numerous affairs of honor on "The Sands" are the following rules:

"Weapons — pistols. Distance — the usual. When the parties are placed in their respective positions on the ground, the word to be given by the second (to whose lot it shall fall, according to custom). 'Are you ready?' and if neither answers 'No,' he proceeds and says 'Fire.' Then, and not before will the Principals elevate their pistols and they may shoot at any time after the word 'Fire' has been uttered — while the Second continues saying 'one, two, three.' When the word has been pronounced, the party who has not before that shot, loses his fire for that round under the penalty which the Law of Honor imposes for infraction of that rule."

There are records of many duels that were fought on the Island — records written in ink so faded it is hardly legible, but most are of so personal a nature that it would be unkind to tell of them. In the Presbyterian churchyard there is cut in the wide stone covering a grave — "Arthur Alfred Gilling, Born in London, England, 1811. Died February 12, 1839. 'Prepare to meet thy God!'" Only a few living today have heard the true story of how Gilling was killed by an Islander in a duel fought on "The Sands." Fewer still know that the inscription was placed over the grave of the young Englishman by the man who killed him. Such was the strange code of honor — at its worst and at its best.

Edingsville, like other places intimately linked with the past, has its phantoms. When the moon is full and the north wind blows, making the waves dash angrily on the shore, a beautiful woman dressed in white walks on the lonely beach; and if one is brave enough to follow her, she can be seen to disappear beneath the waves. It is an accepted fact that over a hundred years ago during a violent hurricane the wreckage of a large ship and the body of a young girl were washed ashore. Services were held for her, and she was tenderly laid to rest close by one of the churches. Islanders are sure that the white phantom is this girl. Occupants of oyster boats passing the Island after first dark often spy her on the beach, looking toward the ocean for her loved ones lost in the depths of the sea.

The late Mr. Cecil Wescoat told many strange stories of the Island. His favorite was one that he himself witnessed. A young girl became seriously ill after she had gone with her family to spend the summer at the Bay. One night at the height of her illness Mr. Wescoat and other neighbors kept watch on the wide veranda. The tide turned and swept out to sea. Suddenly, to the astonishment of all, the sick girl, clad in her night clothes, walked through the door and down the steps toward the ocean and disappeared. Before the friends could follow her, the girl's father came to the door. "My child is dead," he said brokenly. Some of the neighbors rushed down to the beach while others went into the home. Both were bewildered — those who found no footsteps on the ocean strand, and those who looked sadly at the bereaved parents kneeling by the lifeless form of their child.

For years the beach — reached only by boat — has been a mecca for fishermen. The largest bass, trout, and other game fish abound off its shore. Each year, high tides and wind have claimed a part of the tiny isle. Soon the place that once was the scene of so much joyous living, touched at times with sorrow, will have disappeared into the sea as well as into the storied past.

The Churches

IN TELLING of the churches that played such an important part in the life of the Island people, I have depended on histories, the Session Minutes Book of the Presbyterian Church, and Bishop Albert S. Thomas' manuscript history of the Episcopal Church. Unfortunately the early records of the Episcopal Church were burned, so it has been impossible to make the account of this church so full as that of the Presbyterian. It is known that there was an early congregation of Baptists on the Island, but the last church service held by them was in 1774. Both Baptists and Presbyterians worshipped in the same building in 1722. From 1774 on, except for a period when "Mrs. Daniel Townsend's Baptist Church flourished," the white inhabitants of Edisto have attended either the Presbyterian or Episcopal church.

The Island, isolated as it was, had little contact with other churches. There is a story told of one of the old Islanders that illustrates this. Many years ago her daughter, who was attending school in Charleston, became engaged to be married, and the bride-to-be wrote home about her fiancé and of his ancestry, finances, and religion. From all accounts he appeared to be a most acceptable young man. The girl's mother was asked by a relative if she was pleased with the match and the lady replied, "Yes, except he is a Methodist; I have never seen one."

II

According to Ramsay's History, Henry Bowers in 1705 secured a grant of three hundred acres on Edisto and conveyed it in 1717 to certain persons therein named in trust for the benefit of a Presbyterian minister on Edisto Island, but the first page of the present Session Book "established as by-laws of the Presbyterian Corporation of Edisto Island at a regular meeting of the members held at the church" bears the date of August 30, 1790. The Reverend W. S. Lee has written in this book a history of the church during thirty-seven years of his pastorate, 1821-1858. As it is probably the most complete of any record in existence and few people have read it, I am quoting from it.

"In the year 1821 the present pastor was called and took the pastoral charge of the Presbyterian church of Edisto. The elders then in office were Daniel Townsend, William Seabrook, William Edings and Ephraim Mikell.

"In 1836 and '37 three of the elders died, and in consequence of the age and infirmity of the remaining elders four of the members were chosen to the Eldership and ordained in March 1837; viz. W. G. Baynard, William Seabrook, William M. Murray, and J. J. Murray. I. J. Mikell was elected and ordained in 1843.

"Previous to the year 1821, the church had been connected with Charleston Presbytery, but in consequence of some cause, unknown to the writer, it had not been represented in the Presbytery for several years. Before or about 1821 the Presbytery had become extinct by the death or removal of its church members, and this church, therefore, became unconnected with any Presbytery, in which state it continued to exist. The Government in every other respect has been and is Presbyterian.

"At the time the present pastor took the charge of the church there were no sessional records in existence by which it could be determined who were communing members or when those claiming to be such were admitted to the church. Aided by the most reliable testimony that could be obtained, a list of members was made. The members at that time were sixteen white, and seven colored members.

"In the spring of 1822 the Lord's supper administered. The custom of the church had limited the administration of that ordinance to two periods in the year — viz. the commencement of spring and winter. There are now (1858) and have been for many years past, four seasons of communing annually. There was but one public service on the Sabbath.

"When the inhabitants of the Island resorted to the seashore as a residence for health, the Episcopalian and Presbyterian congregations worshipped in an old building which had been used as an academy. Then the Pastors performed the services sanctioned by their respective churches alternately and much harmony and kind feeling prevailed between the two congregations. About 1824, in consequence of the building used by them becoming inconvenient and even unsafe, the two congregations united in erecting a building which was to be occupied by them jointly in the same manner the academy had been. This new building was erected and opened for divine worship; but in consequence of some difficulty that arose respecting the internal arrangement of the building which could not be satisfactorily removed, the two congregations separated. The Presbyterians relinquished the building to the Episcopalians, and before the next summer they had erected a place of worship for themselves. This building from time to time received improvements rendering it neater and more commodious. From this period public services have been observed in the summer and autumn in the morning, afternoon, and evening of each Sabbath until the year 1855 when the evening service was relinquished.

"About the year 1824 an evening lecture was commenced in a private home during the week and in a very short time was conducted in almost every home in the congregation in turn at the request of the families. The number of persons who attended or expressed a desire to attend having become too large to be accommodated in this manner, the services on Sabbath evening which had also been conducted in private homes were removed into the church where the attendance continued to be large. An attempt was made about the year 1832 to have two services on the Sabbath during the winter and spring and a prayer meeting during the week, but the inconvenience connected with the distance to be travelled on short days caused them to be relinquished in a few years.

"About the year 1823 or 1824 a Sabbath school was organized and exercises attended to during the summer and autumn, when the inhabitants were collected together in the village on the seashore. This valuable institution has been continued to the present time. A library of seven or eight hundred volumes presented by members of the congregation to the Sabbath school has been an unfailing source of interest and instruction to the children. The population of the Island, not being large, the number of children in the Sabbath school has always been comparatively small and varying from time to time.

"About 1826 a Bible class for ladies was formed. The studies belonging to it were attended with interest and it is hoped with profit. Various causes arising from changes in families or change of residence by members would at times interrupt or suspend exercises, but the class was kept up for many years. A Bible class for males was also attempted a few years after but did not continue long.

"From the year 1821, regular attention has been paid to the religious instruction of the colored persons in services appointed and performed by them, apart from the white portion of the congregation. At the close of the morning services on the Lord's day throughout the year they remained in the church, and with prayer and praise preaching was united in an extemporform supposed to be better adapted to their comprehension. The attendance on this service has been uniformly good, sometimes very large, and attention during the services appeared to have given each deep interest. All colored persons who offered themselves for membership in the church have been regularly catechised and instructed on each Sabbath before the morning service, and this course has been pursued with them for twelve months or longer if cases seemed to need it before they were proposed to the Session for admission to seating ordinance."

(All plantations had chapels or praise houses for the Negroes with regular services, and the majority preferred to worship there.)

"At the close of the year 1831, an increasing desire for a protracted meeting on the part of the church members induced the pastor to make arrangements for such services.

"At the present time (1858) there are 30 white members but it is difficult to state correctly number of colored members in consequence of those who have been removed from the Island at different times. It is probable there are over 160 now in communion with the church.

"During the past 37 years, the members of congregation have built two parsonages on seashore, one parsonage on Island, one church edifice on seashore, and one church edifice on the Island.

"The contributions for benevolent objects which have been placed in hands of the Session have averaged $600 yearly."

Mr. Lee then gave the names of church members, including the Negroes with their owner's names. His church history ends in 1858, although his pastorate continued until 1872.

During the war, Reverend Lee refugeed at Graniteville near Aiken, along with many members of his congregation. When he returned to the Island, he found the church in possession of Freedmen, who had organized under the name of the Edisto Union Church.

Mr. Townsend Mikell has left an account of the reclaiming of the church. "We got restoration papers from Washington and wrote our old pastor, William States Lee, to come and help," he writes. "The Commandant of the United States Militia stationed on the Island formed in a line with us on the north side of the church and we marched in. I will never forget that Sunday morning — the church was packed even to the pulpit. In the line were the Commandant, Reverend Lee, Pa and his wife, my wife and I, Mr. and Mrs. E. M. Whaley.

"The Negroes were singing lustily when we went in and before the singing stopped, one of the brethren began to pray and before he had finished, another opened the Bible and started to read. Mr. Lee then held up the restoration papers and said, 'In the name of God and by the authority of the United States Government, we are here to reclaim our church!'" It must have been an awe-inspiring moment. Another member of the Mikell family writes: "The two ministers eyed each other. The colored minister from the pulpit gazed down on the feeble white man standing below. 'Pass me up the order for possession.' The order was read, examined and handed back. The minister left the pulpit, marched towards the door, his congregation following, singing as they went."

The Presbyterian Church was designed by James Curtis, a Charleston architect, in the early 1830's. It is one of the most beautiful in the Low Country, and its membership at the time was considered one of the wealthiest. Even though it had only a small number of communicants in 1823, the minutes of March 5 in that year state: "We, the Committee appointed to examine the trustees' account, do report after careful examination we find due on bonds and notes the sum of $20,354.68."

Extracts from old minutes of the church show that many of the planters left the reprimanding of the slaves to the church. "William and Billy, servants of Evans Edings, having been cited, appeared before the Session on charge of having violated the Sabbath and breaking the laws of their master's plantation by clandestinely taking a boat and going to the City of Charleston. They pled guilty to the charge, and professing humble penitence for the offence, it was decided after the moderator had admonished for impropriety of their conduct, no further action should be taken."

"Mr. Ephraim Baynard informed the Session he had good reason to suspect April and Louisia, his servants, of having sold liquor, it was ordered that they be summoned to attend tomorrow for examination and trial."

On entering the Presbyterian churchyard, one sees a tall monument to those lost at sea "forty-five miles south of Cape Look Out on the coast of North Carolina" by the sinking of the "Pulaski"; Reverend James Joseph Murray, Mary Jenkins Murray, Elizabeth Jenkins Murray, Joseph Edings Seabrook, Margaret Seabrook Mikell, Sara Josephine Edings, Sara Ann Edings are the names.

Scarcely a family on Edisto Island escaped the loss of a loved one in the sinking of the "Pulaski." The boat left Savannah on the morning of June 14, 1838. She stopped at Beaufort and Charleston for passengers. The Charleston *Courier* in its account of the tragedy relates: "The 'Pulaski' danced like a thing of life upon the waters of our harbor and under the mighty impulse of steam loomed away from our port on her northward voyage freighted with a living host intent on business and pleasure. Within a few hours, after she proceeded on her way, at 11 P.M. one of her boilers exploded and destroyed the whole of the midship including so much of the hull that the water rushed in with such violence as to sink her in three quarters of an hour."

Some claimed the boat was racing with another, and the boilers became overheated. Mr. Hibbard, the first mate, denied this and said that the accident was caused by "carelessness in not providing boilers with a sufficient quantity of water."

The truth will never be known, but there are records of the suffering of those who were rescued — the anguished grief of a mother who helplessly watched her beloved children disappear beneath the dark waters, the grief of a husband whose bride of a few hours was torn from his arms by a piece of flying timber, and the terrible uncertainty of the

fate of a loved one, endured by those who were separated
and washed ashore or picked up by a passing boat.

Perhaps it is foolish to allow the sorrows of those who
have been so many years at rest to impress you, but even
today, over a century later, some of the details written by
hands long-stilled in death can cause tears to dampen your
eyes.

III

It was nearly a hundred years after the first Episcopal
Church was built in South Carolina in Charleston before the
Episcopalians worshipped at the Parish Church on John's
Island. Then for a time the rector from the parish church
held services every sixth Sunday on Edisto Island. This was
not very satisfactory, however, and a permanent fund was
subscribed for the support of a new church under the name
of "the Protestant Episcopal Church of Edisto Island." The
following men subscribed:

Christopher Jenkins	$888.00	Henry Bailey	$222.00
Daniel Jenkins	666.00	Jos. Fickling	123.30
Jos. Jenkins	666.00	Archibald Calder	444.00
John Jenkins	666.00	Nathaniel Adams	310.80
Isaac Jenkins	555.00	Joseph Fickling	310.80
John Hannahan	444.00	James Fickling	310.80
Benjamin Seabrook	555.00	Paul Grimbal	222.00
Thomas B. Seabrook	444.00	Jerimah Fickling	222.00
Leighton Wilson	444.00	Samuel Fickling	222.00
William Hanahan	444.00	Daniel Jenkins, Jr.	———— *

* No sum is mentioned, probably because Daniel Jenkins, Jr., was a child at
the time.

According to Dalcho's history, "The church is built of
wood and is neatly finished. A chancel has been lately
(1820) added, at the expense of Mrs. Louisa Beveaux and
Edward Bailey. The hangings were the gift of Mrs. Sarah
E. Bailey. The communion plate, consisting of a Tankard,
Paten and two Chalices, was presented to the church by

Edward Bailey and an elegant prayer book by Joseph Jenkins."

The private register of Reverend Edward Thomas, Rector of Trinity Church, Edisto, 1827-1829, is one of the few documents telling of the activities of this first Episcopal church on the Island. In the yellowed pages of this journal, now owned by Edward Thomas' grandnephew, Bishop Albert S. Thomas, one reads of the baptisms, marriages, and deaths of the Island's planters and their slaves.

The congregation was small — at least so the entry for Easter Sunday in 1827 indicates. On that day, seventeen persons, all but three of them women, partook of Holy Communion. Negro communicants, to whom Reverend Thomas preached in July of the same year, were almost as many as their masters. Slaves, mostly belonging to the Bailey family, and one free man, are listed as the Negro members of the church.

The most frequent entries in the register, however, are of infant baptisms; and, tragically, almost as frequent, notices of infant deaths: "Administered private baptism to a sick child of Mr. and Mrs. John Jenkins, by the name of Joseph," the entry for November 3, 1827 reads. "Born October 30th preceding. It died the following night."

All of the planter's wealth could not protect his children from the "malignant fevers" and "summer complaints" about whose cause and cure he knew so little. In all of the Low Country graveyards one sees numerous small headstones, topped by little angels or lambs — mute testimony to the fact that many a prosperous planter lived to find more of his children in heaven than on earth.

About 1840 the Episcopalians built a new church, and during its construction, they worshipped in the Baptist Church at the invitation of Mrs. Daniel Townsend, whose father was one of the first supporters of the Episcopal Church. Although the Episcopal Church was used during the war, first as a Confederate Cavalry headquarters and afterwards as U.S. Coast Survey Observatory by the Yankees, it fared better than the Presbyterian. The Yankees removed the new organ from the Presbyterian Church and shipped it to the North. One of the Northern soldiers carried away the Episcopal prayer book, given by Mr. Jenkins; and many years later a member of his family returned it to the Island. It is beautifully bound and is about eleven inches by eighteen inches in size. The name of the church and the donor is embossed in gold on the back.

Having survived the war, the second Episcopal Church building burned in 1876. The last church erected is on the site of the old. Ancient trees shade it from the hot summer sun and protect it from the gales of winter. They stand guard, too, over the graves of those who first worshipped beneath their overhanging branches.

Yankee Interlude

IT WAS 1860, and with the passing weeks and months the war clouds grew denser. The Edisto Vigilant Association was formed. At a meeting on Monday, October 29, 1860, its president, Honorable John Townsend, addressed the session: "Gentlemen of the Association, as we are organized for the object, especially of protecting our slave institutions, it is proper we should hold frequent council together, and carefully consider the modes by which it might be assailed.

"The crisis is fast approaching and a few brief weeks will decide whether we are to drag out a few years more of dishonored existence under a black Republican rule, which has openly declared their purpose to destroy us or whether casting all unmanly fears to the winds, we shall take our destiny under our own control, and with God to help us, resolve that we will be ruled only by ourselves."

Possibly, Mr. Townsend did not know how fast the crisis was approaching, for in a few short weeks the Secession Convention met, and South Carolina voted to secede. Almost before the South realized, it was at war. Fathers and sons volunteered. In less than a year nearly every able-bodied white man on Edisto wore the Gray of the Confederacy.

After Port Royal fell to the Yankees in November, 1861, the governor of the state ordered all women, children, and disabled men to leave the Island. The majority refugeed Up Country, in Aiken, Orangeburg, Union, Sumter, Spartanburg, and even as far as Pendleton. A great many slaves were carried with them.

The Island became a no-man's land. The fine old houses were left vacant with the furnishings intact. Animals were turned loose to forage for themselves. One of the Island boys, sent out with a scouting party to secure food for the Rebel Troop stationed at Adams Run, wrote: "The hogs, cows, and fowls and other animals left here when the inhabitants deserted are perfectly wild and have increased wonderfully. Our party shot two cows today near Colonel Joe Whaley's place on the Creek — one got down the bluff when wounded and died in the Creek. We continued our hunt through the Island as far down as Edings Bay — started a great many hogs but owing to the want of dogs (we only had two) we only caught one and killed another. The object of the party was to catch, not kill the hogs. We have more beef than we can destroy. We catch the hogs, tie them and leave them to be taken up by the wagons that follow us. It's fine sport hunting them among the sand hills."

The Yankee gunboats came to the mouth of Rock Creek and anchored. From there the Federals could see some of the beautiful homes of the planters, and they came ashore and took possession of them. Strange voices issued orders to

(153)

the frightened Negroes, and unfamiliar people slept in the fine mahogany beds and ate from the priceless china. Vandal hands rummaged through old trunks and chests and scattered sacred belongings.

The Federals left mementoes of their stay on the white plastered walls in the attics of the William Seabrook house, Oak Island, and Cassina Point. Scribbled names of soldiers, regiments, and threats against the Rebels are numerous. At Cassina Point, written in pencil, there still remain the names of the 3rd Regiment, New Hampshire band, and some names of a Massachusetts regiment. One can see in the attic of the William Seabrook house hand-drawn pictures of Jefferson Davis hanging to a tree and terrible threats to others. Is it any wonder the hearts of the owners, when they returned to their beloved homes, were filled with bitterness?

The end of the War between the States found some of the old homes on Edisto Island occupied by missionaries, who had come from the North to teach the Negroes while the Island was in possession of the enemy.

Mary Ames, one of the missionaries, tells in her diary of her life there: "On May 10th at 10 o'clock we left Charleston on the propeller Hudson for Edisto Island. Sailing along the shore and up Edisto River we reached the landing place just at sunset. It seemed like fairyland — everything so green and fresh — the air so soft. We brought on the boat one hundred and fifty Negroes, who, as soon as they landed, built fires to cook their supper. The live oaks in the background, with their hanging moss, had a very picturesque effect.

"We spent the night on the boat, the Captain giving up his stateroom. We had a visit from a Mrs. Webb and one of the officers of the 32nd Regulars — two companies of which are stationed here to protect the Island from guerillas. We were asked to breakfast at headquarters which was about half a mile from the landing.

"May 11: At seven we started for Camp which was on the plantation formerly owned by William Seabrook. They gave us a good breakfast, then the Colonel placed at our disposal a large army wagon drawn by four horses to take us, with our trunks and boxes, to find a place to live. The drive was delightful, the road shaded and cool, winding under immense live oak trees covered with moss, the wild grape was in bloom and the air filled with its perfume. We passed several homes crowded with Negroes."

Miss Ames tells of establishing her residence at Windsor on Russel Creek and of life among the Negroes. Later, the missionaries went to Edingsville for the summer, and she tells of selecting one of the planter's homes to occupy for the season. "When we broke up the pleasant summer home in October we established ourselves at the beautiful Seabrook place." A note of resentment creeps into the diary when orders were received from the Federal government to vacate the planters' homes and return them to their owners.

A tragedy occurred among the missionaries on Christmas Day, 1865. J. P. Blake of New Haven, Connecticut, and Miss Myra Stanton and Miss Helen Kempt of New Bedford, Massachusetts, attempted to leave Middleton plantation, where they were staying, to spend the day with friends occupying California plantation on the other side of St. Pierre Creek. Hours passed and the expected guests did not arrive. Late that afternoon, the bodies of Mr. Blake and Miss Kempt were washed ashore, but only the hat of Miss Stanton was found floating on the water. Three weeks afterwards her body was recovered.

The missionaries were not familiar with the river, and when the small row boat overturned at the first bend in the creek, they were all drowned. They are buried in a far corner of the Presbyterian churchyard. No other graves are near, a low railing surrounds them, and simple stones merely give their names and state the fact that they died on Christmas Day, 1865.

Fishing and Hunting

THE North and South Edisto rivers abound in fish. Up in the brackish waters of the South Edisto many varieties are found. Shad go there in the spring to spawn, and once the huge sturgeon were so plentiful that caviar was shipped in barrels to the North.

Early in the 1870's, Captain John Griffen and John Griffen, Jr., came from Perth Amboy, New Jersey, where their uncle owned a shipyard. They first worked on the jetties off Charleston. The men became so interested in fishing they established a big camp on Pine Island across a creek from Megget's Point on Edisto. Huge numbers of large sturgeon came up the Edisto River to spawn, and the Griffens soon had a large profitable business, shipping caviar North. Captain Griffen bought Meggetts' Point on Edisto Island. His daughter, Mrs. Burns, who inherited the plantation, told me that when she was a child the business was flourishing.

The sturgeon were caught in "Gold Medal" nets made of heavy cord, ordered from the American Net and Twine Company. A large floating pen with high sides anchored off the head of the wharf kept the sturgeon fresh until butchering day, which came once a week.

A thick iron hook, thirty inches long, was used to take the sturgeon from the pen to the wharf, where they were iced to be sent to Fulton's Market in New York. The eggs were put in huge tubs and certain portions of salt added. Mrs. Burns said her father always attended to this, the amount of salt used being a secret he never divulged. After several days, the eggs were stripped from the membrane and put in sieves containing wire bottoms and allowed to drain until fairly dry. The caviar was then ready for shipment. Old account books show it brought the Griffens a dollar a pound.

Sturgeon can still be seen jumping in the South Edisto River, but it has been years since any effort has been made to net them.

❧ From January through March there is fine shad fishing in the South Edisto River, but it is only in recent years that South Carolina fishermen have known that shad will strike a hook. The method used is slow trolling, with artificial bait. A shiny little lure called a spoon seems to attract shad best. To our surprise last spring a fifteen-pound rockfish hit one of these spoons. For many years shad have been netted commercially for two months in the spring.

The fishermen on Edisto, both white and colored, have always claimed that the biggest fish caught on this side of the Atlantic come from the waters that border the Island. There is friendly rivalry even among the natives, and there have been tall tales told of fish caught in the surf, tidal creeks, and rivers. I have seen many evidences of the truth of these tales.

In July and August tarpon feed and play near the shores of the Island. As they leap above the waves their beautiful silvery bodies curve to an almost perfect half-moon before they plunge into the water. Schools of mullet make silver streaks as they dash in front of the tarpon, and literally swim for their lives.

Methods may be different in other localities, but it is just before ebb tide that the fishermen on Edisto start casting for tarpon. Usually, two men in a small boat go offshore about a quarter of a mile and let their lure of live mullet or artificial bait drift with the tide. From our cottage porch we can see an angler when he gets a strike, and it is a signal for us to reach for the binoculars, for we know a battle worth watching is in progress. The struggle will last anywhere from a minute to an hour, although sometimes the "Silver King" makes one leap and throws the hook. Tarpon have no food value, but the fish, from the time it goes into the air at the pull of the hook, is a challenge to a fisherman's skill and patience. Tarpon have been gaffed a mile from where they took the bait, and, then again, a fisherman may beach his boat and bring the fish in alive.

The deer season opens in August, and a drive is held each week on one of the large plantations. The hunters, wearing scarlet shirts or caps, meet at a stated place and wait the arrival of the dogs, which are brought up in trucks. The men are stationed at stands and warned not to leave until a car comes to pick them up. Men who wander off the stands have been mistaken for deer.

At a signal from the driver, who rides on horseback behind the dogs, the pack is turned loose and the drive is on. If it is a large hunt, there are several drivers. Sometimes the wait seems endless, as one slaps mosquitoes and occasionally feels the bite of a wood tick. But when the bark of the dogs and the whoops of the driver are heard, and then come the rustling of leaves, the breaking of dry twigs, and a beautiful, breathless deer pausing a moment before it heads straight across your path, all discomfort is forgotten.

An old custom, followed to the present time, demands that the tail of a hunter's shirt be cut off if he fires at a deer and misses; and when a sportsman kills his first deer his face is gleefully bathed by his companions in the animal's warm blood. The hunters claim the thrill of the kill is worth going through with this penalty.)

In October, winter trout begin to run, and large bass leave the deep cool water and come near shore to feed. The call of the marsh hen echoes across the creeks, and, at high tide hunters have no trouble bringing in their limit of the little brown birds. The marsh hen builds its nest high up in the tall grass to escape the high tide. We found one nest with nine eggs, light brown with darker spots. So cleverly was the nest hidden we would have passed it by, but the hen with a loud squawk arose and flew off. We went quietly away in hope that she would soon return.

In the early summer, creek shrimp are caught in cast nets and small seines. Many call them "Charleston shrimp" and claim they are sweeter than the large prawns caught later in the river. The cast nets are circular affairs about six to eight feet in diameter, with leads spaced on the edge at intervals. They are thrown from the shoulder, usually with a small portion of the net clasped in the thrower's teeth. The Island Negroes make the nets with a hook that is something like a crochet needle, an art handed down from father to son. The thrown net sweeps out like a bird before settling on the bottom of the creek. Cords are so arranged that, as the thrower draws the net up, it assumes a balloon-like shape; the shrimp are imprisoned within the bag. Mullet, too, are caught in this way.

Crabs are in abundance all the year; and if one knows where to look, clams and oysters are plentiful. Along the coast, and in the numerous tidal creeks on the Island, the angler finds drum, bass, whiting, trout, and various other fish — and that rare delicacy, diamond-back terrapin. The summer flounder is delicious, broiled or fried. It is a flat, oval fish, with both eyes on the same side. It has very sharp teeth that often will snap down on your finger even after the fish has been some time out of the water. Flounder are said to reach a weight of thirty pounds, but the average is two to three. It is not unusual for a member of my household to bring in ten to twenty flounders after a few hours "graining" in the creek — a grain is a long-handled short-pronged fork. The flounders are caught after dark, at low tide, as they lie half-buried in sand or mud near the bank. They will take a hook baited with shrimp, but graining is the most popular method.

Wild Life of the Marsh and Shore

IN THE old days a unique breed of ponies roamed over the marshes and sand dunes on Edisto Island. The ponies, called marsh tackeys, were a faded brown in color and were about four feet high. They led a wild, free life, existing on marsh grass, berries, and the leaves of native shrubs. When fresh water was not available the little horses would find a low spot of ground and with their hooves dig holes which became filled with water. The tackeys were excellent swimmers but seldom left the Island. In time of hurricanes or severe storms they instinctively sought shelter and high ground.

When captured and broken to harness, the wild marsh ponies were found to be most useful on the plantation. Pens were built in the marshes and slaves at times were able to drive whole herds into them. At first, the ponies refused to eat corn, oats, or hay, but after a few days they ate heartily and with regular feedings and shelter they improved in appearance until they were remarkably attractive little animals. They would become so gentle that children could ride or drive them. Many lived for twenty-five or thirty years.

I can find no record on the Island of the origin of these strong, sturdy little ponies, although many old letters mentioned them. Some say they were brought by the Indians, while others think they drifted down from the Shakelford Banks in North Carolina near Hatteras — first brought over by Sir Walter Raleigh's colonists. They were as much a part of the Island as the Sea Island cotton, and like the cotton have disappeared.

The Edisto marsh tackeys were once mentioned in the national press: "An old Edistonian planned for his three daughters to break the old custom of successive generations marrying their kin," wrote the *New York Sun* in 1903. "He arranged for his girls to attend school in Virginia and to

(160)

spend a summer, properly chaperoned, at a famous resort. But all three, after many conquests came back to Edisto and married first cousins. 'The tackey will go back to the Marsh,' the old schemer remarked, as he gave away his last daughter to his nephew on the next plantation."

II

Birds are everywhere on the Island. The curlews flock in masses; white terns are like a dense fog as they rise and fall; pelicans fly in formation or single file. Bluebirds and mockingbirds nest near the beach, the beautiful little painted buntings, the most brilliantly colored of our North American birds, are seen in great numbers. In our yard, hummingbirds flit from one oleander bloom to another, and in the early summer one can occasionally see a newly mated pair of somber gray doves. It is a common sight to see swallows, especially in August when they migrate, swooping and dipping parallel to the coast in their flight.

In April a few years ago, while driving along the highway bordering the ocean, I stopped the car to watch a small flock of ducks resting on the water just beyond the breakers. As I watched, an eagle swooped down and lifted one from the water. As the eagle flew inland, it was attacked by another, and the two were soon tangled in fight. The duck dropped in front of my car. When I picked it up I found it was a Ruddy duck, and one leg was broken. As I entered the car, I looked up and saw the two eagles hovering over my head. I carried the duck home, and my husband made a splint for its leg. We hoped to be able to send it in a week or so to join its companions, but it died. We thought the eagle's sharp talons had injured it internally.

Last year a covey of quail was hatched in a clump of tall sea oats between our cottage and the ocean. A cock quail and his mate build their nest on the ground, and they take turns sitting on the eggs. In late spring the call of "Bob-White" rings out over the Island and beach. The birds are quite tame, and it is not unusual to see a pair leisurely crossing the road with their little brood following.

The past spring, ninety members of the Carolina Bird Club spent several days on Edisto, taking pictures of birds. They counted 108 varieties on the Island, ranging from a bald eagle nesting in a tall tree up on the Island to sandpipers on the beach.

Early in the morning or late in the evening, one can see hundreds of white herons perched in trees along the marsh. The trees appear to be covered with a mass of great white blooms. The Negroes say, when herons hover in great numbers during the day it is a sign that a storm is brewing.

III

On moonlight nights in June, the grandchildren clamor to be taken on a turtle-egg hunt. Carrying a flashlight, we go down to the beach just as a tip of the moon appears on the far horizon. There is something eerie about the night and the mysterious feeling the sound of the waves can bring. The children sense it, too; they stay close to me, and the smallest one holds tightly to my hand. We are very quiet as we walk along.

After several false alarms we see the broad track of a turtle's flippers on the sandy beach. It is easy to trail a turtle to its nest; but it is more fun to follow one and watch it make the nest. After we have found the turtle, we are soon joined by other people, and the turtle is surrounded by interested spectators. If she is not frightened, she slowly crawls up the beach, and with her neck outstretched looks for a place that suits her, beyond the reach of the high tide. After selecting it she uses her hind flippers alternately, scooping the sand from under and piling it to the back. Then, with a swing from each flipper, she finishes scattering the sand. The nest, dug to a depth of about ten inches below the surface, is now ready.

I have seen large tears roll out of a turtle's eyes while she lays her eggs. It takes probably twenty minutes for her to lay them, and they vary in number from fifty to two or three hundred. While she is laying them, the turtle seems unconscious of her surroundings; even if a person stands on her back she does not notice it. After the eggs are laid, the turtle immediately covers them with sand, smoothing it evenly over the nest. She then turns around and heads to the sea. I have never seen one lay facing the water.

In the past, Island Negroes ate the eggs and used the yolks in cooking; the white part will not cook hard. Turtle meat is considered a great delicacy, but it is now unlawful to kill turtles or to gather their eggs. The eggs are hatched by the sun. The little turtles, about the size of a silver dollar, just "bubble up" out of the sand and start for the sea.

An old Negro on the Island told me that when he was young the boys considered it great sport to find the turtles and ride them into the water. They cannot bite behind their forelegs, so the children had nothing to fear.

A turtle is covered with a bone-like shell, rounded slightly to fit over the top of its body and marked off with numerous indentures. Underneath each of these sections is a different kind of meat, resembling chicken, beef, fish, or venison in flavor. The flippers are covered with a thick, rough skin. Many turtles live to be quite old and often reach a weight of several hundred pounds.

During World War II, the soldiers who patrolled the beach in front of our cottage often stopped by on their way back to camp, and we would make sandwiches and coffee for them. One rainy night when the full moon lay hidden behind a dark cloud, we suddenly heard two shots. Then all was quiet. Instantly we had visions of a submarine landing, and even though thick black-out curtains were up, we put out the lights. Shortly afterwards, there was a knock on the door, and I heard someone calling my name.

I opened the door, and there were two of our young soldiers — hardly more than high school boys — who had stopped by several times before. They followed me into the kitchen while I was making coffee, and a member of my household asked them if they had heard the shooting. They looked embarrassed and then burst out laughing. Outside, they told us, they had seen something that appeared to be a man crawling along the beach. The boys called "Halt," but it kept going. By that time the boys were thoroughly frightened, and they both fired. Fearfully walking up to the object, they discovered they had killed a large sea turtle.

New Days and Ways

FOR many years the Island was shut off from the outside world, and in its isolation it became sufficient unto itself. Except for privately owned boats, the only means of transportation were such steamers as "Pilot Boy," "Silver Star," "Edistow," and "The Mary Draper" — the last to draw anchor at the old public landings. All cotton was shipped on flat boats pulled by a tug that stopped at the shipper's wharf. Even after bridges spanned the creeks, marshes, and rivers, it was long years before many people from the mainland traveled the road to the Island.

Now the old washboard road has been replaced with a modern paved highway, and the causeway is no longer impassable at high tide. The beach is lined with modern summer cottages, and cars with foreign licenses speed along the highway. Here and there a 'possum, red fox, or 'coon lies crushed by swiftly turning wheels, and sometimes a venomous rattler fails to slither across the road quickly enough to escape a death blow.

A new fishing pier extending a thousand feet into the ocean has recently been built, and the owner also has a modern motor court adjoining his pavilion, across the highway from the pier. Many new cottages are under construction. A broad paved state highway runs parallel with the ocean for several miles.

Plans have been perfected to build a paved road through the jungle, and building lots have been laid off. The state park has an attractive swimming area and a pavilion and several vacation cabins that rent for a nominal sum. Signs of progress are everywhere. Fortunately, the new developers have expressed the desire to keep Edisto a "family beach" and to avoid anything that approaches a carnival atmosphere.

Truck farming and cattle raising have taken the place of Sea Island cotton. Far back from the public road on the plantations where descendants of the original owners live, sleek fat cattle feed on lush pasture land. The broad fields along the highways are planted in potatoes, cabbage, cucumbers, lettuce, and tomatoes. Long ago the historian Ramsay wrote that the soil on Edisto "is favorable to the culture of turnips or green crops." The statement is still true. As quickly as one crop is gathered, the land is prepared for another. Last year the crops were so bountiful, lessees of the land brought in foreign labor to do the work formerly done by Negroes, and the bright clothes of Mexicans added new color to the Island. They came from Texas — from San Benito in the "lower valley of the Rio Grande" — and proved to be efficient, industrious, and well behaved. In the early evening they raised their soft voices in song, accompanied by the picking of guitars. Strangely enough, the gay strains of "Estralita" floating over the moonlit marshes seemed to suit the Island almost as well as "Lookin' Down Dat Lonesome Road."

Up on the Island the ancient houses stand proudly —
some in garbs of glistening white surrounded by well-kept
grounds, others seemingly dressed in deepest mourning, with
sagging porches and weathered walls that have felt no paint
for years. All speak of spectacular grandeur that has passed.

At times, one may hear a woman's happy laugh ring out
in an empty room, and late at night there may come from
long-closed ballrooms the sound of dancing feet. Visitors
claim they are awakened by strange voices — some soft and
gentle — some with the quick Northern accent of the in-
vader. Often there comes the beat of horses' hooves, and
often the tramp, tramp of weary marching feet.

Heavy brocade ball gowns are stowed away in trunks in
attics or in the Charleston museum, and dueling pistols in
their solid mahogany cases are packed away among other
mementoes of the past. But the unstudied hospitality, fine
portraits, and lovely old silver in the homes tell of successive generations of gracious living.

Edisto changes, but somehow remains the same. Today,
there is the hum of automobile tires on the highway and the
bustle of holiday crowds on the beach. But the phantoms of
the past persist. Amid the roar of the ocean surf near "The
Sands" a wave slaps the beach with the sound of a pistol
shot. The gray moss streams from live oaks like plumes from
the helmets of young men dressed in the armor of the
tournament. An old Island resident bows in passing with the
courtesy and the calm assurance of a bygone era. Just as
surely as the flood tide leaves its imprint on the shore, life
marks a land.